www.wadsworth.com

www.wadsworth.com is the World Wide Web site for Thomson Wadsworth and is your direct source to dozens of online resources.

At *www.wadsworth.com* you can find out about supplements, demonstration software, and student resources. You can also send email to many of our authors and preview new publications and exciting new technologies.

www.wadsworth.com
Changing the way the world learns®

An Actor Performs

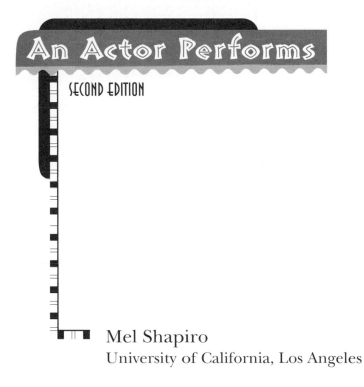

An Actor Performs

SECOND EDITION

Mel Shapiro
University of California, Los Angeles

THOMSON

WADSWORTH

Australia • Brazil • Canada • Mexicoo • Singapore
Spain • United Kingdom • United States

THOMSON
— ✦ — ™
WADSWORTH

Publisher: *Holly J. Allen*
Assistant Editor: *Darlene Amidon-Brent*
Editorial Assistant: *Sarah Allen*
Senior Technology Project Manager: *Jeanette Wiseman*
Marketing Manager: *Mark Orr*
Marketing Assistant: *Alexandra Tran*
Marketing Communications Manager: *Shemika Britt*
Project Manager, Editorial Production: *Jennifer Klos*
Creative Director: *Rob Hugel*
Executive Art Director: *Maria Epes*

Print Buyer: *Doreen Suruki*
Permissions Editor: *Audrey Pettengill*
Production Service: *Sara Dovre Wudali, Buuji, Inc.*
Text Designer: *Patricia McDermond*
Copy Editor: *Cheryl Hauser*
Cover Designer: *Bartay*
Cover Image: *David Toase/Getty Images*
Compositor: *Integra*
Printer: *Transcontinental Printing/Louiseville*

Printed in Canada
1 2 3 4 5 6 7 09 08 07 06 05

Library of Congress Control Number: 2005923110

ISBN 0-495-00719-6

Thomson Higher Education
10 Davis Drive
Belmont, CA 94002-3098
USA

For more information about our products, contact us at:
Thomson Learning Academic Resource Center
1-800-423-0563

For permission to use material from this text or product, submit a request online at
http://www.thomsonrights.com.
Any additional questions about permissions can be submitted by e-mail to **thomsonrights@thomson.com.**

To Jeanne

CONTENTS

PREFACE TO THE SECOND EDITION

Two new chapters on the basics of acting now open *An Actor Performs*. These chapters are designed to assist the beginning as well as the advanced student. Both studying and teaching basic acting can be laborious and agonizing. And boring beyond belief. The teacher asks, "Are you really communicating with each other?" And the partners stare into each other's eyes for about twenty minutes while the rest of the class falls asleep, waiting for someone to say "See, they communicated!" Or the basics can be delivered as a huge box of jargon and terminology. "I felt my sense memory helped me pursue my super-objective because it justified the sub-textual motivation I had actuating the cross to pick up the ashtray." At that point everyone in the class is thinking, "Gee, he really gets the basics!"

But the basics needn't be boring or about jargon at all. One learns a language by being immersed in its sounds, its words and repetitions, the gist of its meaning. The excitement of learning comes through experiencing what it feels like to speak and understand it. Only later are we helped by knowing the details of its grammar or correct syntax. In acting too, it's best to experience first, then put a label on it.

Hence, the basics of acting are presented here through story-telling exercises. And as the storytelling exercises deepen and become richer, more and more of the basics are being put into the mix.

In this edition, I have also added new exercises on developing a characterization as well as two new character research projects. These projects have come out of class and concern themselves with the actor as a social activist. I have been surprised at the degree of passion and commitment students have shown working on "real" issues and presenting them to audiences.

Who knows? Perhaps there's a new theatre in the making after all . . . and it's going to be made by the actor.

ACKNOWLEDGMENTS

I wish to thank Laura San Giacomo, Olympia Dukakis, Ron Leibman, and Allison Janney for their contributions; Rick Roemer for assisting in the manuscript and his good advice; and mainly all those students over the years . . . they were my laboratory and teachers. Thank you also to Barbara Rosenberg.

I would also like to thank the following reviewers for their constructive comments:

Lou Campbell, Belhaven College
Randy Reinholz, San Diego State University
Larry W. Coleman, Wingate University
Lori Kuhn-Hancock, Bainbridge College
Belinda Collings Thomson, Brescia University
David E. Majewski, Richard Bland College
Karla Knudsen, Savannah College of Art and Design
Rocco Dal Vera, University of Cincinnati
Ken Robel, Halifax Community College
Nancy K. Pennell, McPherson College
Stuart Lenig, Columbia State Community College
Diane Hostetler, North Seattle Community College
Michael Kasnetsis, East Los Angeles College
Fredric Wild, Lycoming College
Richard Major, Milligan College
Katheryn White, Saint Peter's College
Kevin Connell, Marymount Manhattan College
William Biddy, Mississippi University for Women
Phoebe Hall, Fayetteville State University
Jim Simmonds, Western Nebraska Community College
Richard Burk, Casper College
Frances Pici, Georgia State University
Cindy Stover, Metropolitan Community College
Mark Frank, Coffeyville Community College
Kurt Edwards, Indiana Wesleyan University
Frank A. Barnhart, Columbus State Community College
Gregory Justice, Virginia Polytechnic Institute and State University
Karen S. Martin, Miami-Dade College, Kendall campus

Charles Falcon, San Antonio College
James M. Brandon, Hillsdale College
Sharon Andrews, Wake Forest University
Jane Brody, Louisiana State University
Jim Bartruff, Emporia State University
Carol Schafer, Pennsylvania State University
Andrew Longoria, Mansfield University of Pennsylvania

INTRODUCTION

This book is about how actors use the world of imagination to achieve a performance. It is about using imagination to explore the text, using imagination to open yourself as an actor, and using imagination to search for the essence of the character you're performing. This book is for beginning, intermediate, and advanced students of acting. It is also for working professionals with many years of experience. The difference between the levels is made by skill and knowledge gained from experience. But the problems on all levels are the same: understanding the text, finding a viable interpretation, dealing with the language of the play, and using one's body and mind and imagination to create a fully realized performance in the part.

This book is called *An Actor Performs* in the belief that the actor, during an exercise, a scene in class, a rehearsal for a production, and finally on stage, is always performing. The best work is the work that is "out there," being performed. Actors shouldn't be thought of as having an internal Cuisinart in their psyche that grinds down their own experiences for them to pour back into their own veins for the benefit of only themselves. Unless those experiences are performed, they remain unexpressed, uncommunicated, and of what theatrical use?

This book is divided into five parts.

Part I deals with the tools. The basics of the craft are explored through the use of storytelling and improvisation. From there we move on to the creative use of the actor's biography, techniques for reading and analyzing plays, an awareness and usage of language, and skills in making effective acting choices.

Several years ago I developed an exercise called "autodrama." I felt that many young actors thought that "acting" or "performing" is something that you apply on top of your own self or put on like a mask at Halloween, that acting is getting up there and strutting around, using fancy language, being larger than life, and generally imitating bad acting. I wanted the actor to know that he or she could be simple, honest, autobiographical, and theatrically viable without laying on a lot of effects. Autodrama has become the first exercise I do with a new class, whether it's a group of precollege students or a group of seasoned professionals. As you develop skills in using your own experiences, it is very important to understand that you must develop your reading and text analysis skills at the same time. All this goes hand in hand along parallel lines.

It's surprising how few acting classes deal with text. The assumption is that because students get a smattering of text analysis or play reading as freshmen or sophomores, they should know it! It doesn't work that way. Play analysis is usually not taught from an actor's point of view, and unless it is ongoing and integrated with acting, total amnesia on the subject occurs in the senior year. As long as acting students and teachers are content to believe that reading skills are not a part of an acting book or an acting class, we are training actors who are one hundred percent dependent on their directors and teachers for "interpreting" the text for them.

Art, like life, is about solving problems. You have to experience the solution for yourself so you can solve the problem when it comes up the next time. The irony is that while others are making both your artistic and intellectual choices for you, you are the one who's going to be on stage doing the performance. And if you really can't read a text in a way that opens it up to your own imagination and helps you own the role, what you end up giving the audience is an empty result. I hope the chapters on Reading the Text (Objectively), Language, and Reading the Text (Subjectively) will help you become a contributing member of the production team.

Part II is about the process. Process is the slow, developmental growth of layer upon layer of autobiography, text skills, and acting technique into a way of working. The key to having a way of working that connects the tools into the process is imagination.

The exercises in this book are designed to extend the actor's imagination into the world of the play and into the private experiences of the character. The actor needs to create a bridge from himself to the character and back again. How do you relate to the character? Are your life experiences analogous? What if they are not? There is a series of improvisations and exercises that can create as much useful memory as experiences you might have lived.

Part III explores putting together the work done on the use of tools and process into characterization, which is where all roads eventually lead. Living the life of your character through particular improvisations, exercises, and research techniques is illustrated. A system of asking yourself certain questions, asking your character certain questions, and using a diary is examined in detail.

Extending the actor's range via comedy, one-person shows, cabaret, performance art, and research projects such as the Activist Project constitutes **Part IV**. These areas can be viewed as advanced work. However, they can be encouraged as extracurricular activity or can be approached at the same time as other work is taking place. (There are times when I wonder if work on comedy and cabaret should not be the beginning of actor training.) These areas go to the heart of actors' empowering themselves. An idea whose time has come.

Part V is an interview with four actors on the nature of performing on stage and on camera. The actors are Ron Leibman, who won a Tony for Best Actor playing Roy Cohn in Tony Kushner's *Angels in America*; Olympia Dukakis, who received an Academy Award for Best Supporting Actress for her work in *Moonstruck*; Laura San Giacomo, who made her film debut in *sex, lies,* and *videotape*; and Allison Janney, four-time Emmy award winner for the television series, *The West Wing*.

Most chapters end with a FAQ (frequently asked questions) session to summarize the points that have been discussed. These questions have all been asked in one class or another, time and again. Asking questions is one of the ways you learn to teach yourself.

My personal philosophy is that no one can teach you how to act. All the teacher can do is help you teach yourself because art is a slow, self-taught process that goes on for the rest of your life, or as someone once said, "Art is in the becoming."

But before we talk about art, let's talk about reading and its importance. Theatre is a branch of literature, the best of which is continually performed as the repertoire. What the audience comes to see is a story on the stage, seemingly told by actors. Actors have to know the repertoire, but more importantly they have to know how a play is built, what its structural elements are, how its story is technically being delivered, and what makes one play different from another.

It is not necessary to have read the plays cited in the exercises and examples to use this book. The extracts should be clear enough. The following plays are recommended reading. Those italicized are cited in this book.

Aeschylus	The Oresteia
	Agamemnon
	The Libation Bearers
	The Eumenides
Sophocles	*Oedipus Rex*
	Antigone
Euripides	The Bacchae
Aristophanes	Lysistrata
Kalidasa	Sakuntala
Chikamatsu	The Love Suicide at Amigima
Machiavelli	The Mandrake
Shakespeare	*Romeo and Juliet*
	Hamlet
	Twelfth Night
Racine	Phedre
Moliere	Tartuffe
Aphra Behn	The Rover
Congreve	The Way of the World
Goethe	Faust (Parts I and II)
Ibsen	*A Doll's House*
Strindberg	Miss Julie
Wilde	*The Importance of Being Earnest*
Checkhov	*The Sea Gull*
	The Cherry Orchard
Wilder	The Skin of Our Teeth
O'Neill	*Long Day's Journey Into Night*
Williams	*A Streetcar Named Desire*
	Cat on a Hot Tin Roof
	The Glass Menagerie
Hellman	The Little Foxes

Beckett	*Waiting for Godot*
	Endgame
Brecht	Mother Courage
Hansberry	A Raisin in the Sun
Genet	The Maids
Orton	What the Butler Saw
Pinter	The Homecoming
Jones	*Dutchman*
Churchill	Cloud 9
Wilson	The Piano Lesson
Mamet	*Sexual Perversity in Chicago*
Shange	*for colored girls who have considered suicide/when the rainbow is enuf . . .*
Fugard	*"MASTER HAROLD" . . . and the boys*
Guare	*Bosoms and Neglect*
Kushner	Angels in America
Sondheim, Gelbart, and Shevelove	*A Funny Thing Happened on the Way to the Forum*
Guirgis	Jesus Hopped the 'A' Train
Mee	Big Love
Durang	Betty's Summer Vacation
Cruz	Anna of the Tropics
McNally	Love, Valor, Compassion
Auburn	Proof
Parks	Topdog/Underdog
Heaney/Sophocles	A Burial At Thebes
McDonagh	The Pillowman

ABOUT THE AUTHOR

Mel Shapiro is head of acting at UCLA's theater department. He was one of the founding members of NYU's School of the Arts Theatre Program, where he taught acting and directing for many years. Later he became the head of the drama department at Carnegie Mellon University. He has taught acting privately in New York and Los Angeles.

He has directed on Broadway (the musicals *Two Gentlemen of Verona*—Tony and New York Drama Critics award, Best Musical—and *Stop the World*), off Broadway for the Lincoln Center Repertory (Vaclev Havel's *The Increased Difficulty of Concentration*—OBIE award, Foreign Play), the American Place Theatre (*The Karl Marx Play*, by Rochelle Owens), and had a long association with Joseph Papp and the New York Shakespeare Festival (John Guare's *Marco Polo Sings a Solo* and *Rich and Famous*, John Ford Noonan's *Older People*, and Shakespeare's *Richard the Third*). He directed the original production of Guare's *The House of Blue Leaves*—New York Drama Critics, Best American Play—in New York. He has directed at many regional theatres including Arena Stage in Washington, DC, the Tyrone Guthrie Theatre in Minneapolis, MN, the Center Theatre Group in Los Angeles, CA, and the Eugene O'Neill Playwrights Conference in Waterford, CT. His production of Charles L. Mee's *Big Love* ran five months with the Pacific Resident Theatre Company in Los Angeles. His work has been seen in London, Paris, Berlin, Amsterdam, and Tokyo; and in Canada at the Royal Alexander, Toronto, the Stratford Festival, Ontario, and the Citadel in Edmonton.

Mel's work as a playwright is just beginning to appear in regional theatre in the United States and Canada. He founded *The Journal,* which is the magazine of the Society of Stage Directors and Choreographers, and has served as an artistic advisor for the Fund for New American Plays, administered by the John F. Kennedy Center. He is the recipient of the Tony, OBIE, Drama Desk, New York Drama Critics, Los Angeles Drama-Logue and Joseph Kesserling (first prize) awards. He is also the author of the book *The Director's Companion.*

An Actor Performs

PART 1

THE TOOLS

Among the tools the actor has to work with are:

- The basics of the craft: talking, listening, concentration, improvisation, playing another's story, tapping into emotions, theatricality

- Personal biography—how the actor begins to use his or her life to create a theatrical event

- Skills in reading a play objectively—understanding some of the basic elements of structure to see the play as a whole and to understand the author's intentions

- An awareness of language and how language shapes character—exercises to develop skills in activating images and verbs

- Skills in reading the text subjectively—how the actor begins to see the text as material to be played on the stage and how to make choices that are actable

THE BASICS IN ACTION

Watching a fine swimmer, you can admire the form, the line, the coordination, the flexibility, and the control and use of the body. With that control comes the speed, the power, and seeming ease of the performance in the water. How did the swimmer get to such a point? She might have been born a talented athlete, but it took years of drilling the basics to get where she is. Hours in the water, working on stroking, rotating, aligning the body, kicking, timing of breathing, varying the pace, building stamina, practice, hard work, love of the challenge.

Acting, too, is built on learning, experiencing, and finally mastering the basics. The basics are beautifully simple, completely logical in their way, and like a sport, demand the following of the student:

■ Giving up of ego. Accept what you don't know and be ready to learn. Take criticism and being corrected positively, knowing that you can't progress without it.

■ Determination. There's no such thing as failure; there is just picking yourself up and getting on with it. You have to be nonjudgmental about yourself and others around you.

■ Enjoy the bumpy roads. Not every exercise is pleasurable or easy. Some may be difficult, out of your range, or scary. Those are the ones you need to work on the most.

■ Learn from others. Watch, listen, stay tuned to what is going on with actors around you. Process their experience as well as your own.

■ Keep a notebook and record your observations.

Embedded within the following set of exercises are many of the basics. The exercises are done with examples, and the student and teacher should feel free to invent their own variations on them.

Don't worry about terminology. All that will come eventually. For now, experience the process first. Ask questions later.

TELLING STORIES

Acting is a form of storytelling. A play is a story told by actors. Our lives are a long series of stories. We tell stories about ourselves, about others; we tell stories that are true and others that are near fiction. And we listen to the stories of others.

Let's find the basics of acting through the context of storytelling.

Exercise 1: A Simple Story

The group sits on chairs in a circle. Going around the circle, each person talks for three or four minutes about his or her day so far—what happened, what didn't happen, how eventful or boring it's been, and so on. It is important no one feel the need to be interesting, or funny or tragic. Simply be yourself (whatever that is) and really talk to the group. Muttering or talking into the floor should be avoided.

Everyone wants to hear what you have to say.

Goal: To be simple in telling your story. You don't have to push or impress anyone.

Exercise 2: Find a Little Drama

This time talk about the most interesting thing you did recently. "Interesting" does not have to have been a major earthshaking event. Sometimes the smallest things in life are the most interesting and the most meaningful. Or you might recall something dramatic that has happened to someone you know.

Goal: By now you are relaxing and becoming familiar with each other as a group and hopefully enjoying listening to each other. People might feel they haven't started "acting" yet, but that's all right.

Exercise 3: Telling Someone Else's Story

After everyone has done the preceding exercise, someone should be chosen at random to tell another person's story. This is always an electrifying moment. Will Sue remember what Molly said? Was she listening? Sue proceeds and with only a few variations is remarkably able to reconstruct what Molly said, if not in detail, then in gist.

> **Goal:** Not only to only talk, but to listen. To tune into what is being said, and in many ways, how it's being said.

Exercise 4: Spinning into Invention

Now that Sue is telling Molly's story, Larry is asked to continue where Sue left off. Of course, he doesn't know how Molly's story continues because Molly didn't go that far. So Larry has to make it up. And at any critical juncture, he can pass the story on to the person next to him.

> **Goal:** You have gone from talking, to relaxing with each other, to listening, to going from fact to imagination. You are beginning to see how fictitious events are within the realm of what people will believe. (Is this acting?)

COLORING THE STORIES

We've all made a story better than it is by spicing it up, adding rain when it was just a drizzle, not only talking about the rain but experiencing it once again in our bones, using our bodies to act it out.

Exercise 1: Add an External Circumstance

This circumstance could be a weather condition, a time of day, or an event that's taking place. Sue told the group how she missed the bus to class yesterday, misplaced her cell phone, and had no way of contacting anyone to report she would be late. Tell her story adding the element of rain. Try doing it as though it occurred during a snowstorm. Try it during a heat wave.

Goal: You can see how external circumstances condition your behavior and how much more focused you become because of them.

Exercise 2: Act without Words

Molly gets up and acts out her version of Sue's story. She runs for the bus, misses it, searches for her phone, all the while getting soaked in the rain.

Goal: This is the first time you have gotten up to perform for the group. Try telling the story physically and see how it feels. Use words only if absolutely necessary. After doing it in real time, try it in slow motion, focusing on the details.

Exercise 3: Stressful Moments

Tell of a time when you were in an extremely difficult physical situation. For example, you broke a bone during an athletic event, you were hospitalized for some reason, you were lost in the snow, or you were badly sunburned on the beach. Talk about it; describe it in detail. Now let another student in the class act it out.

Goal: Did the person acting out the scene convey the pain you felt? If not, you may not have described it specifically. If it wasn't specific, how well did the actor convey the pain anyway?

Exercise 4: Which Story Is True?

Act out two short episodes you think are interesting. However, one story happened, the other is fabricated. Can the group guess which is which? You can use words, but sparingly.

Goal: Because you always want to act like it's the truth, no matter how far out or exaggerated the tale, it should never seem you are unbelievable.

EMOTIONAL STORIES

When the actor is asked to express big emotions in an exercise, it is perfectly fair for the teacher or director or others in the group to ask, "Did you really feel such and such?" "Weren't you faking?" Don't worry about that now. Just try to get the feelings out. Don't edit yourself, or nothing will flow.

Exercise 1: Phone Calls

Reproduce a telephone call you either made or received that was highly emotional. Go through the incident.

Do a phone call where something unexpected happened.
Try a call where you tell something that is very difficult to say.
Receive a call that made you very joyful.

Goal: Start thinking of yourself as an orchestra that can play many different notes, colors, and expressions. Try to get to the emotion quickly.

Exercise 2: Portraying Another's Experience

Each person does his or her variation on another person's story. It's as though you are exchanging lives. (Is this acting?)

Goal: Capture the essence of the drama as you understood it. Be careful not to go into parody or caricature the person you're basing your version on.

Exercise 3: Fantasy Call

A call you've always wanted to make. Something you wished you said, but didn't. That call you always dreamed of comes in.

Goal: Free yourself on this one. Any emotion, any way you want to express what is happening is fine.

DIFFERENCES IN STORYTELLING

Exercise 1: The Narrator and the Performer

One of the actors in the group (Sue) invents an improv for another actor (Larry) to carry out. Larry acts out whatever Sue tells him. Sue wants this scene to take place in a living room, so several chairs and a sofa are set up. She needs a phone, newspapers, a window, and a door. Those too are set up. She will stand to the side and invent a scenario. Larry is ready to go to work, not knowing what Sue has in mind. She begins:

Sue: You come through the door screaming like a maniac, throw yourself on the sofa, get up, throw yourself on the floor, and keep screaming and kicking until you wear yourself out.

Larry looks at her for a moment, then hurls himself into the action. He crashes into the room, almost breaking the door and howls and kicks and goes to the sofa and tries to beat it up, rolls onto the floor, and kicks until he's exhausted.

Sue: Now take the newspaper and tear it to shreds.

Larry tears the newspaper in shreds, then even smaller shreds.

Sue: You are sobbing uncontrollably. Go to the window and try to jump out.

Larry goes to the window, crying uncontrollably.

Sue: No, don't jump. Better idea, go to the phone, laughing hysterically.

Larry suddenly giggles as he goes to the phone.

Sue: Laugh more.

Larry laughs more.

Sue: Cry.

Larry cries.

Sue: Laugh and cry at the same time.

He tries.

Sue: You dial your mother. You're crying again. A lot.

Larry dials. He tries to talk, but the crying gets in the way. Finally.

Larry: Mom, mom, it's me, Lar'. Mom, oh, mom. . . .
Sue: Suddenly you're frightened. Throw the phone away. Run
    out of the room.

*Larry screams in terror, drops the phone like a hot potato, runs into
the door, falls down, gets up, and runs out.*

Goal: Each actor is working off the other's imagination. The
actor performing the improv jumps from emotion to emotion.
Some he hits and some he misses, but he tries to respond to the
given stimuli as quickly as possible. Keep inventing different
scenarios as each group member gets a chance to perform.

Exercise 2: The Narrator and the Performer, Continued

Tom has been fascinated by a true story Mike told to the group
earlier. He asks Alan to act it out while he narrates. Other than
the fact the previous exercise was pure fiction, notice another
important difference in this one: the use of motivation. Here are
the steps suggested to Alan:

  Tom: You've had a car accident. Your front wheels skidded on
    the wet road and you banged into a parked car. You

walked half a block to your apartment, cold, wet, with your
neck and shoulders in pain. You enter the room.

Alan goes through all the following.

Tom: Come in and deal with the pain somehow.
Tom: You want to take your wet jacket off, but can't.
Tom: You're almost on the verge of tears.
Tom: You're supposed to pick your parents up at the airport in
an hour. Call Betty, maybe she can help.

Alan dials, lifts the phone to his ear, and feels the pain.

Alan: Hey, Betty, can you help me out? My folks are going to be
at United baggage waiting for me at noon. I had an accident, all four wheels on the slick road, and I crashed into
a parked car. No, I don't know whose, I didn't have time.
I left a note. I need a ride to the airport to pick up my
parents, can you help me? You can't? Oh, no, what will
I do? No, they don't have a cell phone, I have no way of
reaching them. . . .
Tom: Hang up. Get Phil's number. It's in your book bag
somewhere.

*Alan finds his bag, rummages through everything, can't find the
number.*

Tom: Call the airlines, page them, do something fast.

Alan goes to the phone.

Tom: There's a sudden twinge of pain from your shoulder to
your neck, like an electric current, it's like you are being
electrocuted. You scream.

Alan howls in pain.

Tom: The phone is ringing, you try to get to it, you can't move.
Try to get to it, Try . . .

Goal: We are now given reasons, or justifications or motives, for what the person is going through, unlike Exercise 1 where the emotions are arbitrary. Take note of an interesting development:

Alan is doing *things (calling friends, working through his pain, trying not to fall apart) because of what* he wants *(to have his parents not stranded at the airport and worried about him) due to his* circumstances *(his accident).*

Note: The differences between the exercise with Larry and Sue and the one with Tom and Alan is almost a difference in certain styles of theatre. The first improv, Exercise 1, might be described as more free-form and nonliteral, where things happen arbitrarily and for no apparent reason and where it is ultimately up to the audience to fill in what's missing.

The second improv, Exercise 2, is more in the style of theatre, film, and television performing today. This is where human behavior is presented in seemingly real, understood, and motivated ways. We can clearly identify with the trouble Alan is in and watch his struggle as he works himself out of it.

■ ‖ ■ ‖ ■ ‖ ■ ‖ ■ ‖ ■ ‖ ■ ‖ ■ ‖ ■ ‖ ■ ‖ ■ ‖ ■ ‖ ■ ‖ ■

FREQUENTLY ASKED QUESTIONS

Q: Why do you state so strongly the actor shouldn't mutter or talk into the floor? Can't I just speak softly?

A: Right from the beginning open your voice, inhale, and let the breath out as you speak so that you are connecting to what's inside you. Twisting everything back down into yourself is like switching a motor off, not on.

Q: I feel I'm not being honest that way. You said to make things simple.

A: Not being heard is not honest either. It's completely artificial. Watch people telling stories and you'll see what I mean.

Q: From what we've done so far I see talking and listening are among the basics, is that correct?

A: Yes. Is listening hard for you?

Q: Sometimes I concentrate so much on listening I'm not hearing a thing.

A: You should have a need to listen. Hear what's interesting to you, what you can relate to, what you can use. . . .

Q: When we added the elements such as rain I was in and out.

A: What do you mean by that?

Q: Sometimes I felt the rain, but then my concentration got focused on something else and I thought, "Oops, I'm not feeling the rain anymore." How do I correct this?

A: I'm glad you brought up the words *concentration* and *focus* because nothing is more basic. The issue is always what to concentrate on. The physical situation becomes a great given in the scene. The rain makes you feel wet and cold and annoyed, and increases your frustration at whatever you are trying to do . . . in this case attempting to find your cell phone. And once you've established the reality of the rain, the audience is going to wonder where it went when you've dropped it. Has the sun suddenly come out?!

Q: I got a lot out of the slow motion exercise. It was like I was living in a more detailed way. Everything became much more vivid to me.

A: Also it was the most relaxed I've seen you. You had the urgency the scene demanded, but you were very much at ease. Your breath came naturally; you enjoyed letting your body do the work.

---

continued on page 14

continued from page 13

Q: In a number of exercises you encourage the actor to use as few words as possible. Why?

A: I really mean to say to use words only if you need them. It is counterproductive in an improv to get into playwriting. You always want to stick to the task and do what's necessary to achieve it. If babbling endlessly is part of the task, fine. But a lot of dialoguing in an improv is a digression and sometimes is just plain old-fashioned showing off.

Q: The exercises where I had to put out certain emotions, or jump immediately to them . . . I kind of liked them because I didn't know I could go from one to another like that. But isn't that what they call "playing for results," just emoting on cue?

A: That's right. That's the exercise.

Q: So it's okay to do that?

A: Yes, because it was the exercise, not a rule of life. Don't forget you did the variation with justification as well.

Q: When I was doing the work on remembering how certain events felt, how that phone call made me feel, when I had to relive telling someone something that was very hard to say . . . I found a lot of that personally difficult. Yet I enjoyed getting to those places. Will we be doing more of that?

A: Yes, over and over.

Q: When you relive an event, what's it called"

A: Let's call it "Using Yourself."

Q: Is that one of the basics?

A: Absolutely. Ready to move on?

Q: Ready. But one more question. Is there some criteria we should use when commenting on each other's work in class?

A: Base your comments on what worked and what did not work for you. Mainly question anything you didn't understand. Stay away from value judgments such as, "That was pretty bad," or "That was great, fabulous."

Q: We should be supportive, no?

A: Supportive in understanding you're all in this together and can appreciate another person's growth. But no fake supportive "you're so wonderful, give me a hug" nonsense from either the students or the teacher. Let's be honest, to the point, and as clear with our comments as we can. That's truly supportive.

MORE BASICS: WORKING WITH PARTNERS

As we continue exploring the basics, this section might have been subtitled, "Playing Together: Ten Exercises." But right now I can hear some groans in the background. "More basics? I want to act, I want to do scenes, I want to do monologues, I want to work on audition material to help me get a job in stock this summer! When do we act?"

We have been acting. And now we're going to focus on working with partners. As for audition material, we will not be doing that. But we'll discuss acting in plays at the end of this chapter.

Once again, the following exercises are in the form of improvisations. Some of these exercises need preparation between the partners before they are done. Of course, the improv itself can't be rehearsed, otherwise it ceases to be improvised. And it must be reiterated that a whole lot of talk is not necessary in any of these exercises. No playwriting please! And if you must be clever and funny all the time, stop concentrating on the audience and concentrate on your partner for a change.

PLAYING TOGETHER

Exercise 1: "Hey, Is This You?"

Cast: A male and female

Who you are: Yourselves

The situation: You are sitting close, facing each other. Close your eyes. Each person gently feels the other's face, hair, neck, shoulders. Describe how the other person feels, what sensations come from the touch. Music plays. Eyes open. You get up and dance, but not with each other. However, your whole focus is on the other person. You can stay apart, or weave in and out of each other, or touch for a moment.

16

The acting problem: To be focused on the other person and to respond to whatever nuance, vibration, or attitude you receive. Don't push anything. Perhaps a *want* may happen. See where it leads. You may want to be gentle with the other person, or he or she may want to challenge you . . . see where it goes.

Exercise 2: Moonlight Serenade

Cast: A male and a female

Who you are: A modern-day Romeo and Juliet

Preparation: Think of a number of songs, either classical or popular, dated or current, that you can use. It does not matter if you are not a good singer.

The situation: A wooing scene with songs. Either height or distance separates the lovers. He sings a few lines of a song to her. She responds by singing something to him. They sing back and forth, either keeping the same songs with different intentions, or finding other songs to respond with.

The acting problem: He wants to woo her. She wants to be wooed but is not convinced of his sincerity. He wants to show how much he loves her. She needs to know she's not just another pickup. All in song. And if you don't know any, try doing the scene to "Happy Birthday."

Exercise 3: Marooned on a Desert Island

Cast: Two or three actors

Who you are: Yourselves

The situation: You don't know where you are or what happened. You've been here for four days. You're hungry, thirsty, and have no equipment, phone, or baggage. You are three people who didn't much like each other to begin with.

Preparation: The partners need to work out the details about the island, the temperature, how long they've been out of food, and anything else they think pertinent.

The acting problem: Take your time in the situation. Find how you are going to survive being together and on this island.

Stay away from the back story, which is how all this happened.

You do not have to resolve this situation. See where you get in ten minutes.

Exercise 4: A Date Gone Bad

Cast: A male and female

Who you are: Yourselves

Preparation: The actors need to work out the details together of exactly what happened before the scene begins. Whatever occurred may or may not be revealed in the actual improv. But the actors have to know what happened.

The situation: A parked car in front of the girl's house. Late night.

The acting problem: You liked each other a great deal, but whatever happened is now an obstacle to your relationship. Do you want to continue seeing each other, or let each other go? Do not prejudge the scene: let the decision or indecision happen as a result of the playing.

Exercise 5: Parting with Something of Sentimental Value

Cast: Two actors

Who you are: Yourselves

Preparation: One of you brings in something that may not be very valuable, but is very important to you. A ring, a watch, a signed autograph.

The situation: A's dog is ill and needs to be taken to the vet. But A is broke and is trying to raise $25 for the visit. A asks B to buy the object. But even though B is willing to buy it, he does not want to pay the selling price. Unless A gets that price, it's pointless to sell.

Acting problem: I need to sell it. I want to buy it. How do I get my price?

Exercise 6: Turf War

Cast: Four actors
Who you are: Avid tennis players
The situation: A and B play at a certain time and place every Sunday. A arrives five minutes early only to see C and D getting ready to play. C and D tell A they reserved the court by phone with the park manager and hence it's theirs for the hour. A disputes this. B arrives, finds out what going on and refuses to leave. Both teams want the court as no other time is available.

Acting problem: To find as many possible ways to get the court from the other team. You can threaten physical violence, if it comes to that, but do not use it!

Exercise 7: Rivals

Cast: Two actors
Who you are: 17-year-old high school students
Situation: Alan is having lunch. Ben asks permission to sit at his table. As they eat, Ben wants to know if it's true that Alan is asking Mary Lou to the prom. Alan says it is true. Ben announces he intends to ask her. Each wants to take her, each believes he's the one she prefers, and each wants the other to back off.

Preparation: Before the improv, the actors have to clarify who Mary Lou is, what she looks like, and what their relationship to her has been. The scene suggests eating is going on. This may help you with the scene. Carefully think out how you are going to incorporate this.

The acting problem: It is possible that each man knows something about her the other does not know. Don't tell the other actor in advance what that is. Remember, you are both 17-year-olds.

Exercise 8: Bargaining

Cast: Two actors
Who you are: 10-year-olds, very temperamental
The situation: Each of you has a "precious" comic book collection. You often swap and trade, but you always feel the other

person is cheating you. Try to get back at your friend by getting the most from him and giving the least. Try to get his most valuable comic book.

Preparation: You'll have to bring in comic books, or some kind of substitute. But their presence is key.

The acting problem: you are 10 years old and should behave accordingly. Hint: anything goes if it's in service of getting what you want.

Exercise 9: An Indirect Approach

Cast: Two acting students

Who you are: Basically yourself

The situation: The class has been assigned to do a contemporary, two-person scene. Steve wants to work with Ellen. He feels she is the best actor in the class and would be great to work with. Ellen, however, prefers not to work with Steve. She feels he's a little unreliable. But she does not want to hurt his feelings.

Preparation: The actors must know the plays they will be discussing.

The acting problem: Ellen has to get out of working with Steve without hurting his feelings and preferably without directly telling him she won't work with him.

Steve has to be very sensitive about Ellen's feelings in the sense of not pushing her where she doesn't want to go, but getting her to work with him.

Exercise 10: The Provocateur

Cast: The entire group

Who you are: Opinionated students

The situation: Someone in the group who has a strong political, social, or moral stance on war, race, sexuality, crime, education, or other issues tries to get as many people in the group on his or her side. Opponents of those views should try to rally support for their side.

Someone in the class acts as referee and gives points to the best arguments. The side with the fewest points takes the winning side to lunch.

The acting problem: Many people don't like expressing their views on certain issues. But in this case you need to win the lunch. Take a side even if you are not convinced of it yourself. The danger of the exercise is that things can get personal and hurtful. It's important to keep this in mind and apologize after for behavior that went too far.

IT'S TIME TO DO A PLAY

The purpose of this exercise is to serve as a diagnostic. The teacher and the students can begin to assess what has been learned once it is put into another kind of practice: the written text replaces the improvisation. Customarily the student will enter this area via two-person scenes or monologues. There are many fine published ten-minute plays, however, that have the virtue of being complete unto themselves; hence, the actor gets to experience the progression of a role from beginning to end. Some of these plays are no more than extended skits, or superficial comedies. But others are quite powerful and contain some juicy roles for actors.

The danger in this kind of exercise is that the student will forget the Basics and start acting up a storm and revert to old habits. It could also be argued, "They know nothing about rhythm, timing, character, structure yet!" All that may be true, but how long can a person practice tennis strokes without being thrown into a game? If the work on the ten-minute play is treated as work in progress and not as a major test of an actor's talent, much can be pulled together and learned.

Here are some suggestions for working:

1. The actors who have decided to work together should carefully read as many of these pieces as they can.
2. Then, short-list their favorites and have a reading to see which one they prefer.

3. Make sure the roles are equal. One character doing all the speaking while the other has very little to do is not a fair choice.
4. Set your rehearsal time realistically. Often people look at their calendars and see they have nine hours free during the next two weeks, which is when the scene is due. But they think with juggling and squeezing they have found more time, say fifteen hours, which sounds much better than nine. But as the week goes on, they find they can't drop this and that, or other things replace them unexpectedly. So here's what happens. One of the partners starts canceling, which makes the other partner upset. Or, someone is continually late to rehearsal. Therefore, set your rehearsal time together based on what you know you can do and not what you would like to do.
5. You are responsible to each other. No lateness, no failure to show up.
6. Use rehearsals productively.

   a. Do not direct your partner. You'll have enough to do acting your own role.
   b. Start with reading the play several times.
   c. Discuss what you think it's all about. If you disagree, that's okay. Work it out rationally.
   d. Set a deadline for when you will have learned the lines.
   e. If props are required, decide who is going to bring them.
   f. Make sure you run-through the whole piece three or four times before presenting it.

7. You should be able to invent improvs by now that will help you with various aspects of the play, or to help yourself with certain acting problems you are having. Use rehearsals as a discovery process. For example:

   a. Sit down with each other and tell your character's story as it occurs in the play.
   b. Talk about what happened to your character before the play began and what might happen after the play is over.

c. Make sure you are listening and ask questions based on what you are hearing about this character.

d. Find a piece of music the characters might move or dance to. Without words see how you relate to each other.

e. Drop the actual lines of the text, and use your own words. Then, see whether you are keeping the same degree of listening when you return to the text.

8. Keep other people out of your rehearsals. The partners want this to be their work and their effort alone.

■ || ■ || ■ || ■ || ■ || ■ || ■ || ■ || ■ || ■ || ■ || ■ || ■ || ■ || ■ || ■

FREQUENTLY ASKED QUESTIONS

Q: What if I don't like my partner or we just can't work together?

A: Has that happened?

Q: No. But what if?

A: It's been my experience that the work is more important than personalities. The work comes first, personal stuff has to stay out of it.

Q: In some of these exercises you've said not to playwrite, or keep all that happened previously out of it. But won't the audience be confused if they are trying to follow a story and not know what's happened before?

A: We are not doing anything for an audience. You are doing this work for yourself and your partner. You do not focus on the audience unless that is a demand of the exercise. The class is where we do things that an audience is not allowed to see. A class is our laboratory. "No visitors allowed."

continued on page 24

continued from page 23

Always keep the challenge of the exercise in mind and try to achieve it. Try to forget anyone else is there, except whomever you're working with.

Q: Many of the exercises we are doing seem to result in a lot of fighting. Is that what you want?

A: What do you mean?

Q: It always seems to be, "I want versus what you want" and then we fight over it. Or argue, or debate. I mean it always ends up in some kind of conflict.

A: What you are describing is very much like a situation in most plays. Characters want different things and as a result there's a conflict . . . or fight, as you put it.

Q: So fighting is one of the Basics?

A: Finding the conflict is. But several improvs did not end up in what you call fighting.

Q: True. A few ended in a compromise, and the improv based on the date that turned out badly . . . was quiet, not fighting really, well fighting . . . kind of . . . yes . . . it was still an unresolved argument.

A: Tell me about the bargaining exercise where you were 10 years old.

Q: I felt very liberated. I found myself feeling very impetuous and didn't care how selfish I became.

A: That was the intention. As a rule, playing like children will release emotional inhibitions and make you feel very free. Try it on different kinds of material.

Q: I was very offended by some of the statements people made during the Provocateur exercise.

A: Offended, why?

Q: Some of the politics being espoused were sickening. I could barely take it. When I hear some of these people going on about sex, religion, society I could puke! I hate their values!

A: What if you had to play a character whose ideas and values offended you?

Q: That's a different story.

A: Why?

Q: Because in that case I'd be acting. I'm talking about these people in real life.

A: My advice to you is stop being offended and live with it. What you espouse can be viewed as being equally offensive. Art is hard enough. We don't need the thought police to monitor it.

Meanwhile, let's expand and deepen what we've been doing as we move into the next part of the work.

AUTODRAMA

Autodrama is an exercise designed to bring the actor's biography on stage. It's based on the premise that art is essentially autobiographical. When Gustave Flaubert was asked where he got his ideas for Madame Bovary, he would say, "Madame Bovary, c'est moi." The art of acting is no exception. It starts when the actor begins exploiting feelings, memories, dreams, and fantasies that he or she has experienced. Later, when the actor plays the character, there is a bridge between the life of the real person and the life of the fictional one. Some people might believe that acting has no relationship to the actor's life, that it is an act of complete imagination, that the only bridge is between what the actor imagines and what the author has imagined to become the character. I think that all avenues are possible, but I mainly believe that the actor's life is a great tool for acting and can be creatively exploited. What's the point of having lived through all that we have if we can't put it into our work? The autodrama attempts to put your own experiences into your work, first as an exercise, then as a tool in the acting process. In a way, the autodrama permits you to exploit certain areas of yourself so you will know a little more of who you are as you are trying to become who your character is.

A WARNING

Directors and teachers are not physicians; actors are not patients; audiences aren't voyeurs. All too often things happen in the classroom that have no business happening there. A student is encouraged by the teacher to relive some trauma, which provokes tears, hysteria, and emotional upheaval. After which the teacher or director announces to the group that the actor has had a "major breakthrough" and now is the better actor for it. Sadly, though, breakdowns are not "breakthroughs" because the actor will rarely be able to apply what's just happened within him or her to a scene. And now the actor has to deal with what's been dredged up and should have remained buried in the first place.

The teacher or director is not a trained doctor and has mistaken emotional display for drama and has used someone else's pain for his or her own idea of what acting is all about.

USE JUDGMENT

The only person who should derive pleasure from pain is the actor. If you dip into areas of your experience that are painful to you but you know you can use in your work and really want to use, go carefully. You are the only one who knows what you can handle. All too often when actors, especially women, are asked why they let their teacher or director push them into either emotional or sexual abuse, they reply, "I thought it would make me a better actor." You also need to ask yourself how far you're willing to go to please the teacher.

Years ago I asked Herbert Berghof if he did "private moments" at the HB Studio in New York. He said that when he heard that Strasberg was doing the exercise, which consists of doing publicly something you do only in private, he decided to try it. He announced the exercise to his class and the following week came in to see the results. The first student got up, went on stage, and urinated. I asked Mr. Berghoff what he did. He said, "I got up and screamed, 'That is not art!' And that was the end of private moments at the HB studio!"

Three Dangers

1. Teachers or directors who push the actor into psycho-traumatic areas that neither they nor the actor can handle—but the actor willingly subjects himself to for the sake of being a better actor—are opening up

a Pandora's box for themselves, the student, and
the class.
2. Displaying certain experiences for shock effect only becomes
the subtext of the class. "If they are stunned by what her
parents did to her, wait until they hear about mine!"
3. As soon as the actors glom onto the fact that the teacher
is looking for tears, breakdowns, hysteria, or emotional
catharsis, traumatic experience runs rampant.

However, the benefits of the exercise can far outweigh any lunacy
connected to its implementation.

THE AUTODRAMA EXERCISE

Perform what you believe to be the high points of your life in ten
minutes. You can use lights, sound, film, video, other actors, props,
costumes, or you can keep it as simple as you like.
You must fulfill the following three conditions:

1. The presentation must be extremely personal. If you
know that you are going to enter emotionally difficult
areas of your life and that it will cause you pain, avoid
them. But if you believe that the pain is something you
would like to exploit because it's an area that might be
useful to you later in your acting, try it.
2. The presentation must be theatrical. You cannot stand
there talking to the audience like a frozen puppy. Find
a metaphor for your life, such as: "It seems I've been
waiting tables my whole life." In that case, do your life
from the time you're born waiting on tables.
3. The presentation cannot go longer than ten minutes and
should not be less than that. This stricture is to help the
actor give the piece a coherent shape and to prevent
rambling.

The presentation can be scripted or improvised. Referring to
notes during the performance is permissible.

Examples

1. We were locked out of the theatre until the actor was ready. When we were finally permitted entrance, we could see the fellow sitting stark naked on a chair at the far end of the stage. All along the front of the stage were articles of clothing. The lights dimmed, and the actor began to speak. He said that when he thought of the major moments in his life, he thought of the outfits he wore. He got into a pair of short pants and began his first recollections: his mother, his school, being mischievous. He got into his first pair of long trousers, recalled that event as well as many others. He kept overlaying or discarding clothing as his life went along: the outfit he wore at his first prom, the outfit he wore when he first had sex, and so on. These clothes became a Proustian madeleine of memory. One bite and he was back in another time, reliving feelings, people, events.

2. The next piece was equally striking. A young woman announced that her whole life was a series of ill-fated love affairs. With an accompanist, she went through highlights from birth to divorce, all done to torch songs. The actress not only was able to tap into a very deep well of personal loneliness, but she also showed how absurd all her situations were. Before this I had thought her a clever light comedienne. Who knew what was really inside her until she chose to bring it out?

3. Recently an actor brought in a film projector and ran home movies of his youth. He showed us his enviable childhood. But secretly he had always wished his parents would divorce so he could be like all his other friends who were children of broken homes and were caught in the middle of ugly custody battles. He always felt he wasn't interesting enough. Finally, he got his wish. His parents divorced, and he became "one of the boys" and the recipient of lots of attention. However, aside from feeling guilty that he wished his parents' divorce, he realized while doing the exercise that he tends to play

situations in life like jokes and is compelled to skim every surface for easy laughs. He understood this was his problem as an actor: go for the joke, entertain the audience, and keep away from anything he really feels.

Limiting the Exercise

1. Sometimes these exercises get into emotionally disturbing areas that the actor cannot control. One actor was portraying the way he had been tyrannized by his father. He played himself, then played his father. Suddenly he broke down. I asked him to stop trying to do the scene. Afterward he said he got a great deal out of the exercise, even though he was unable to finish.

   A month or so later he presented a monologue from Sam Shepard's *The Curse of the Starving Class* in which a young man recalls his father coming home in the middle of the night, dead drunk, and abusing the family with violence and stupidity. The actor's emotions seemed to come from his remembered experience, which he was now fearless in handling. Probably because he was playing a character. He was letting the character rent his own experiences for the monologue.

2. Again, this is not an exercise only for advanced students or professionals. I have tried it when teaching a class of high school students who wanted to be actors and found their work to be freer than that of older students. It seemed that this exercise was the first time that many of them had had the opportunity to express who they were and what had happened to them.

Additional Autodrama Exercises

1. Create two autodramas. One is from your life. The other is totally from your imagination. Perform them both. See if your group can tell the difference.

Invariably truth is stranger than fiction, and the
autodrama that the audience thought too bizarre to
be anyone's life usually turns out to be someone's life.
2. When working on a play, do your character's autodrama.

■ || ■ || ■ || ■ || ■ || ■ || ■ || ■ || ■ || ■ || ■ || ■ || ■ || ■ || ■ || ■

FREQUENTLY ASKED QUESTIONS

Q: Why is this exercise so terrifying to me?
A: Because it demands that you expose certain areas of
yourself. It also demands that you come up with
something theatrical. What's most terrifying is that
you, the actor, have to make the choices in both
areas, and actors are accustomed to having others
make choices for them.

_____

Q: What if I go over the ten minutes?
A: You'll be asked to stop.

_____

Q: I understand you want the high points of my life. But
what if I have no high points? What if my life has
been ordinary and dull?
A: Do the ordinary and dull.

_____

Q: But I'll be boring.
A: Have a little actor's courage. You don't have to
entertain the audience. You don't have to please
the audience. You just want to perform it, get it out
there, express it as fully as you can, communicate it
warts and all.

_____

Q: But why would the audience want to see me, hear
about my life?

continued on page 32

continued from page 31

A: It's not about the audience. The exercise is about you. It's about what you have experienced, what you have felt. Keep the audience out of it.

Q: But then why perform it? Couldn't I just tell you?

A: You're performing experiences that you will eventually perform behind the mask of a character. Performance is the key to autodrama: You are shaping some of the life you have lived into a theatrical event of your own invention.

Q: What if my ten minutes shock people? What if they hate me after they see what I've done?

A: You have to be honest with yourself and work from your own sense of personal integrity. Predicting other people's reactions and wanting to be liked will not help you get to the places in your work you have to go to.

Q: What are those places?

A: Using yourself and using your imagination to create the life you have to live on the stage.

Q: Are the contents of these exercises confidential?

A: Yes. The group is asked not to discuss them or to gossip about them. An atmosphere of trust is essential.

READING THE TEXT (OBJECTIVELY)

The audience comes to the show because it wants to see a good story performed by good actors. Most actors believe that it's their job to develop good performing skills and that it's someone else's job to provide the good story. This is fundamentally true. Actors aren't expected to be writers. But as we've seen in our work on the basics, actors can be inventive storytellers through improvisational necessity. Actors are also storytellers of a different kind. The way the written story is transformed from the page to the actor's imagination and becomes the character is all one piece. It would be excruciating to listen to a soloist who hasn't fully read the part as he sits down with an orchestra and tries to perform a concerto. Imagine a dancer who knew her choreography but was barely attentive to the musical score. Actors continually learn parts after a cursory reading of the play—if they've read the play at all—and go flying on sheer instinct and the belief that inspiration will hit them the moment they set foot on the stage. Instinct is good. Inspiration is better. But there's nothing wrong with a little old-fashioned preparation before the audience takes its seats.

Ask a college senior about play structure and he'll tell you, "I have those notes somewhere." At least he has the notes. The problem is that no one has required him to use that information in three years. The situation is similar to that of vocal music teachers who are obsessed that their students make the right sounds. What the students are singing doesn't matter as long as the notes are perfect. In acting, too many teachers care only about the emotional life of the moment. As long as the student is yelling, screaming, crying, or carrying on it makes no difference what the text is. When you're working with a singer and you say, "Let's break down the lyrics of this song by Mr. Sondheim," she will look at you like you've lost your mind. For her the lyrics are a vehicle for hitting pretty notes. However, the audience wants to hear the lyrics, laugh at the jokes within them, and appreciate the point of the song. Songs are about content as well as sounds. This is why the actor has to read the play fully, reading with particular skills. Before you even begin to ask, "Who is this character, how does he feel, and how do I play it?" you have to ask:

> What story is being told?
> How has it been put together?
> What's it about?

READING FOR CONTENT

In order for you to begin reading for content, I suggest that, if you have the following habits, you try to break them:

> Scanning the script for the size of your role and reading nothing else
> Highlighting your role with a Magic Marker and dealing only with those words
> Using monologue or scene study books and never bothering to read the play that the material came from

If, at an audition, the director or producer wants to discuss the play with you and you are unable to, you will not get the part.

If, in rehearsal, the other actors and the director are talking concepts and ideas that the play generates and you have not done your homework, then you will lose their respect. If, as an actor, you don't do all the work, you have to question what you're doing in the room.

An actor begins by reading the play, then interprets both the play and the role for structure, content, and meaning. The performance becomes how you see that text, how you finally imagine it. Just as a conductor's performance of a piece of music in a concert is referred to as his "reading" of the score, the actor's performance of the text, to a certain extent, is another kind of reading.

FIRST READING OF THE PLAY

Sit down quietly and read the play in its entirety. Make this first experience with the author a personal communion. You want to receive the play fully. Read it for enjoyment and let your responses flow. Don't think about your role. As long as you're thinking, "Me, my part, my role, how big, how small, how many laughs, where can I make them cry, his part is bigger, she has the last speech, I die in the first act!" your ego will lock you out of the experience of receiving what's truly there. Encounter the play whole, without judging yourself in it.

Remember that this initial encounter with a play may be the only time you will be left alone with it. You will have your teacher feeding you information and opinions, your director giving you views and concepts, the designers giving you theirs, and so on.

STAY AWAY FROM YOUR PART

Read the play several times. You'll probably have questions. Jot them down. It's very important that your questions do not go unanswered. Those questions are the seeds of the actor's work. You are trying to understand the whole play. Actors often tend to see the play only in terms of their own role. Forget that. Understanding the situation of all the characters is the only way you can eventually answer the question most vital to you: "Where does my character fit in?"

There is another reason not to jump into your part but rather to look at the play as a whole mosaic of actions and interactions: The more you concentrate on you and your part at first, the more you will end up on the stage acting by yourself. In life we act and interact with others. We weave a complex network of interplay between each other. This is what you have to look for in the script. All the characters: how they fit together. All the characters: how they are necessary to the story. All the characters: how their story gives meaning to the audience. Therefore, keep these first readings objective: Submit, submerge, surrender to the text.

FACTS AS KEYS

Actors have a tendency to jump to a complete interpretation of the play before digesting the facts that are contained within it. Slow down and collect as much information as you can. A good reader is a good detective: You have to solve the mystery given clues and evidence. The mystery you have to solve is not "who done it?" but rather "what is it?" What is this play about? Of course, the actor has an additional burden. After you have solved the mystery of the play, you have to solve how you are going to act it. But too many actors jump in, ready to act before they know what they are in, what it's about, and how it's been put together.

SOME FACTS TO LOOK FOR

The Title

Why did Chekhov call his play *The Sea Gull?* Someone shoots a sea gull. Later Nina compares herself to one. Should you do some research on sea gulls? The play takes place on a lake. Are there sea gulls on a lake? Does the term have more than one meaning?

Cat on a Hot Tin Roof is a great title. What does it mean? Maggie refers to herself as that. Does that mean the play is only about Maggie? What does Tennessee Williams mean by the image? Maybe all the characters in the play are like a bunch of cats jumping on a hot tin roof.

In *"MASTER HAROLD" . . . and the boys,* you'll notice that its author, Athol Fugard, put quotation marks around the words *"MASTER HAROLD."* Three dots follow (". . ."), *"and the boys"* is in lowercase letters. The world of the play is in this title. Uppercase letters for the master, who is white; lowercase for the boys, who are black. The racial connotation is right there, with *"and the boys"* ignominiously following the *"MASTER"* by three dots. Three dots are like three links of a chain that the master has his slaves tied to. And *"MASTER"* in quotation marks, which refers to a young man, can be taken ironically.

Length, Act, and Scene Divisions

This is the form the story takes. A Shakespeare tragedy in five acts and many scenes allows for much more diversity of character, plot, and subplot than a two-act play of Samuel Beckett, which is highly economical because it leaves unsaid what Shakespeare freely allows to be verbalized, yet it can be equally tragic and universal. Be aware of the scope of the story. Hamm in *Endgame* might be as complex a role as that of King Lear, but the actor has to know that he has far less stage time to create a comparable portrait.

Time

Over what time span does the story take place? Does the situation change, or does it stay the same? Is the action continuous, or does it take leaps forward, or go backward, or jump around? In rehearsal you'll hear someone say, "Wait a minute, it must be a year later, because she's talking about her baby!" Intervals of time have to be carefully noted and examined for progression, regression, or changes. Trepleff has ostensibly become a different person between the end of the third act and the start of the fourth in *The Sea Gull.* Nina has become a professional actress and a mother. Time, however, seems to have solidified Mme. Arkardina's personality—she hasn't changed at all.

Place

Would the same story have happened in another location? What is the locale? Indoors, outdoors? How many specifics regarding place does the author suggest? Is the action of the play at a certain place or at a series of places? Why?

Pinter's stories usually take place in rooms. Often in one room. It's as though the characters inhabit only one room of their minds. It often is a room that is claustrophobic, where very little has to be said because so much is understood between the characters. The actor has to let himself into that room. If he does, he lets in the audience, too.

In the opening of Chekhov's *The Cherry Orchard*, a play whose plot revolves around the loss of a family estate, its owners are in their old nursery, reminiscing. Chekhov could have set the start of the story anywhere, but the nursery is a remarkable image that lets us watch his characters behave in this very particular location. You get the feeling early on that these people cannot deal with the future, let alone with the present, and don't have much of a chance at saving their own property, or growing with the times.

Physical Atmosphere

Weather conditions might be a very important factor in the story. The heat in *Cat on a Hot Tin Roof*, the rain in "*MASTER HAROLD*," the wintry afternoon close to Christmas in *A Doll's House* all need to be recognized as integral to their stories. Heat—combined with tedium and impatience and a longing for something to do—is the spark that ignites the feuds in Romeo and Juliet. Granted, actors and directors can certainly change the atmosphere. An actor might want to play the dueling scenes in Romeo and Juliet in the rain. But the facts connected to atmosphere as originally intended by the author should be very helpful in understanding the work, whether you change them or not.

Conflict

Opposing goals and desires create the conflict in a story, especially a dramatic story. There can be collisions, battles, and titanic clashes on the stage. There can be disagreements displayed in words, such as quarrels, debates, and controversy. Or there can be very subtle conflict that arises from the ways characters make each other feel, which is unspoken, but as powerful as any overt battle.

In "*MASTER HAROLD*" there is seemingly no conflict for a long time in the script. There is the appearance of tranquillity, lively debate among friends, and a certain amount of teasing. All of this is designed to show the audience a "perfect" world before it is shattered. The conflict enters incrementally. The boy is the master and white. The black men are "boys" and can never forget it. Their conflict is inevitable.

In *A Doll's House*, Ibsen builds a subtle network of conflict inside a domestic situation.

1. The minute Nora has to hide her macaroon we see that she is not permitted something she wants. Her husband does not want her to eat sweets. Nora resolves the conflict by eating the sweets and lying about it.
2. Nora tries to be the person her husband wants her to be. Can she achieve this goal? Does she want to achieve this goal? She decides to have it both ways: She can surreptitiously do what she wants and let her husband think she is doing what he wants.
3. Finally comes the most interesting conflict of all: She is conflicted within herself because in having it both ways she can never express who she really is. Nora is condemned to play the doll-wife to her husband, just as she played the role of doll-daughter to her father. Ibsen stacks the cards so that Nora finally has to resolve these conflicts: her duty to her family versus her duty to herself.

Obstacles

Examine the play in terms of what stands in the way of each character getting what he or she wants.

Nora's main obstacle is money. Had she enough money, she would not have forged her father's name to a loan. Had she enough to pay off Krogstad, she would not be in so much trouble. Money is a very tangible and easily recognized obstacle. But a character can have obstacles that are difficult to perceive at first.

What are Helmer's obstacles? Doesn't he have everything he wants? A new job as manager of the bank, financial security at last, a lovely wife, children, and a home. As much as he loves Nora, his cherished doll-wife is an obstacle: She eats sweets, spends too much money, is not practical, gets in the way of his business plans, and so on. And why are these traits obstacles? Nora is such a lovely, vivacious woman, what more could he want? He wants perfection. He wants the perfect wife, the perfect marriage, perfect children, and perfect servants in a perfect house that will shine perfectly in a world he's trying to perfect. An imperfect world will, obviously, conflict with such a goal.

The External Event

Most stories deal with an event that triggers all the action or incidents of the play. An event can be a great war that is taking place, a sale of property that is imminent, a father who must marry off his shrewish daughter, a woman who comes to live with her sister and brother-in-law, a birthday party, a promise that Godot is coming today. All stories are triggered by an event, an event that is taking place or about to. Sometimes an event has just occurred and the action of the play is its aftermath, as in Beckett's *Endgame*.

Examples

1. Antigone has gone against her uncle's decree and buried her dead brother, creating offstage an event that precipitates the play. In other words, this event causes the play to happen.
2. In *The Sea Gull* several events launch the action of the play: A mother returns home with her new lover; her son prepares for a staging of his play, and everyone seems to be on the verge of romantically pursuing someone else.
3. In *Waiting for Godot* the story concerns waiting for an event to take place. Its not taking place becomes the event.
4. "*MASTER HAROLD*" begins with two black men preparing for an amateur dance contest. It is raining. Hally

arrives after school at the teahouse. Small events. Almost ordinary. But there is the suggestion that Hally's father, whom Hally hates for being a drunkard and disabled, may be coming home from the hospital. The father's homecoming, which progresses from rumor to fact, is the event that makes the play happen the way it does. It ignites the story.

OTHER FACTS IN THE STORY THAT THE ACTOR CONSIDERS

1. What is the age of the characters, if given? (How old is Nora?)
2. What is the occupation of each character? (Does Nora have a job?)
3. How is the characters' free time spent? (This is Nora's problem.)
4. Is their love life mentioned? (How do Nora and Helmer answer this?)
5. What are their prejudices and passions? (Nora likes money. What about her passions other than macaroons?)
6. How clear is the social, political, or historical setting of the story? (A woman leaves her children and husband—what was it like then? What's it like now?)

Putting all this information into context, the aim is to see the play from as many points of view as possible and not to see just the actor's role.

HOW IS THE STORY BEING TOLD?

Certain techniques of storytelling will affect your choices as an actor. It is important, therefore, that you make yourself aware of the following.

Tone

There are times after you have read a play when you will ask, "How was I supposed to take all that? Was it a comedy, or a tragedy, or a farce? I had heard that it was funny, but I didn't laugh once." The tone should let you know. It is the mood or emotional atmosphere created by the writing. Now this mood or atmosphere can change in the course of the evening, even in the course of a scene. But how the audience is supposed to take the show is set early on by the writing. The musical *A Funny Thing Happened on the Way to the Forum* opens with a song titled "Comedy Tonight." The song is a cheerful, witty romp, which lets you know that you are going to see a musical farce and that it's okay to laugh. Until that song was put in, the audience was not so sure. However, with contemporary writers, such as David Mamet, John Guare, and Tony Kushner, the tone keeps shifting. The mood of the evening can go from funny to horrifying to absurd to tragic and back to funny. These transitions are roller-coaster rides that the authors, with the help of the actors, put the audience on.

Point of View

In a film, when the heroine suspects something creepy going on in the basement, she gets her flashlight and goes down there. The camera shows us the stairs and the movement of the heroine descending them, the flashlight illuminating various areas, a cat leaping out of the dark, and so on. We are seeing things from her point of view. Some of the points of view that a play can have are:

1. *Hamlet* is certainly written from the main character's point of view. We see the world from his eyes.
2. Sophocles's *Antigone* is written from the point of view of both Creon and Antigone. Each is right, and each is wrong.
3. Bernard Shaw, Luigi Pirandello, and Ibsen often wrote plays from a multiplicity of viewpoints in which everyone's argument was valid and all the contradicting viewpoints added up to the truth.

4. Chekhov seems to have kept his own point of view to himself. Like the doctor he was, he showed his characters clinically and objectively.
5. Arthur Miller and many modern American and British playwrights demonstrate their personal critiques of society and morality.

Plot

The terms *story* and *plot* are often used interchangeably, and this is not correct. Story is the outline of the events. *Hamlet* is the story of a young prince who struggles with avenging his father's murder. The plot, however, is the arrangement of incidents that make up the story in a much more complex way.

Example: *The Sea Gull*
Two people are on a bench, talking of love. He loves her, she loves someone else.

Workmen appear and seem to be setting up for a play.
They leave.
A young man and an old man enter.
They talk about the young man's play, his hopes and dreams.
The young man seems angry at his mother, but very needy of her at the same time. He plucks a daisy. "She loves me, loves me not." A young woman enters and is nervous about the part she must play, and so it goes.

Reversals

Reversals are twists and surprises that happen during a story, moving it forward to its inexorable conclusion. Aristotle believed that the most dramatically effective reversal was when a great man experienced a loss of some kind. A poor man becoming rich did not fit that definition then. But today it does. Examine the story for shifts of fortune or major upsets. *A Doll's House* has an abundance of reversals. Helmer's good luck is set up at the start of the play. He's riding high with a new job. His fortunes reverse when he finds he's being blackmailed. But this is in turn reversed when the blackmailer withdraws his threat. Helmer is riding high once more until Nora leaves him.

Recognition and "Inner Events"

Recognition comes when the character sees something for the first time or understands something in a new way or becomes aware of a reality or a truth. It is an event experienced by the character, usually onstage, and observed by the audience. Juliet wrestles with her ambivalence in the potion speech. She is afraid and confused. But when she envisions her dead cousin Tybalt stalking Romeo, she drinks the contents of the vial Friar Laurence gave her. Recognizing a horrible threat to Romeo is the stimulus that provokes Juliet's action. And just as there are major external events such as feuds, duels, killings, and banishments, there are small events (no less major), which might be called "internal events," those recognitions or perceptions that happen in the mind of the character and that can change the course of the play, depending on what choice the character will now make.

As you are reading the play, look for how the action is changing and why. Look to see how the characters are changing or remaining the same. How much of a progression has there been from beginning to end? And especially watch those very delicate "inner events" that have subtly altered the behavior, aims, and state of being of the characters.

Example
When Helmer learns that Nora has had dealings with the man who is now blackmailing him, he actually tells her she is not fit to raise his children. At this moment, Nora's recognition is that she is married to a man who cannot stand by her and who probably does not love her enough. And this recognition provokes her revolutionary choice at the time: she must leave.

TRUTH AS A CENTRAL THEME IN DRAMA

Since *Oedipus,* truth has been a central theme in drama. The mystery of the story is solved when the truth is revealed and recognized. *Oedipus* is a great detective story. Who is responsible for this plague? Is this a curse? Who killed Laius, the former king? Oedipus says he will find and punish whoever is to blame! Ironically, it is Oedipus himself. He murdered his father, sleeps with his mother, caused the plague. When he recognizes the truth, he tears his eyes from their sockets.

Nora's first entrance is a metaphor for her life: She hides certain things and reveals others. Everything she does, especially for others, must be hidden or lied about or kept a secret. She has been pushed into a life of covert actions that get her into a lot of trouble. So much so that she believes she will have to kill herself. The play is built on the necessity of finally telling the truth and recognizing the consequences.

■ ǁ ■ ǁ ■ ǁ ■ ǁ ■ ǁ ■ ǁ ■ ǁ ■ ǁ ■ ǁ ■ ǁ ■ ǁ ■ ǁ ■ ǁ ■ ǁ ■ ǁ ■

FREQUENTLY ASKED QUESTIONS

Q: And all these facts that I will find in my objective reading of the play—the title, length, time, place, conflict, obstacle, events, specifics of the characters as well as elements of the story such as tone, point of view, plot, reversals, recognition, and truth as a theme—eventually will help me how?

A: They will help you in the next step, which is to find acting choices that work for the play.

Q: What can help me beyond reading?

A: Taking notes, jotting down questions, doing research on the author, finding commentaries and reviews of the play. Discussing the play with anyone who will listen.

continued on page 46

continued from page 45

Q: Other than the elements of story you suggest, what else should I look for?

A: Write what you think are the high points of the play. Write what you think the play is about: the boss versus the unions, one's loyalty to family versus one's loyalty to a mate, Hollywood corrupts, the innocent are always destroyed . . . find the big issues that give the play its thrust.

Q: I feel like I should write a PhD dissertation on all this.

A: Not at all. Your writing should be succinct and to the point. You do not have to be clever. Do not overintellectualize, because all good plays have a core that is very simple. It's the delivery that's complex.

Q: Internal events. . . . I don't know if I've got it straight. Nora in *A Doll's House* goes through a lot of recognitions, a lot of awareness of who she is supposed to be, and finally who she is. All of these psychological and emotional developments are "inner events." Right?

A: Right.

Q: All of which leads to the big climax. Nora leaves her family and modern drama is born! (Someone said that once.)

A: So what are you having trouble with?

Q: *The Sea Gull.* Trepleff's suicide. Big climax. Were there any recognitions or "inner events" that precipitated it? All I see is another long speech by Nina. Then, he goes off and shoots himself.

A: Nina realizes that through all her trials and tribulations in working to become a good actress, what matters most is not having fame or glory but rather knowing that "how to endure and have faith" is more than just words. For the first time Nina knows what she must do with her life. It's a fresh, new understanding that happens at the moment, and which ironically affects Trepleff in the worst possible way. He understands he hasn't the faith to go on.

Q: We'll be working these ideas through a specific acting process, right?

A: Yes. But let's not separate how we act from how we read. They have to be intertwined.

Q: What about language? The author's use of words and how the actor must deal with them.

A: That's next.

5

LANGUAGE: THE MUSIC OF THE PLAY

After exploring the text objectively but before dealing with it subjectively, we have to discuss language, which is a principal tool of both the playwright and the actor. Using words is to the actor what using the body is to the dancer. The language the author has chosen is highly selective and rarely arbitrary. Language creates a style as well as a form to contain the play's content. Put very simply, it's what the actor acts. You can act to silence, and you can act by movement alone, but for the moment, let's deal with the language of words.

Every good piece of theatrical writing is a kind of poetry, whether the characters are speaking in verse or prose. Consequently, the actor must do two things regarding language: recognize its use in the play and develop a technique for its delivery.

Before you begin to read the play subjectively, that is, before you consider how you are going to make choices to act the role, get a feel for the author's use of words. You might want to read the whole play out loud to yourself, playing each part, reading the stage directions. (For the time being don't deal with a play that is in translation.) As you begin to hear the play in your ear, you will be able to say it. In other words, just as a musician takes in the notes on the page and produces them with his instrument, you read the words and produce them through your self (which is your instrument).

LISTENING EXERCISES
FROM REAL-LIFE STUDIES

1. Listen to what people are saying and how they're saying it. For example: Sometimes people will tell things—painful things—that have happened to them in the most offhanded way. It's almost like they are trying to distance

themselves from their own feelings at the time because they don't want to break down.

2. Try to get people to talk. Listen to their imagery as they tell a story. Pay attention to their choice of words.
3. Listen to how people tell a joke.
4. Ask yourself, "What is the engine making this person talk? What is her *need to speak?*"

Documenting People

1. Find someone whose story you believe is worth preserving: a grandparent or a person you admire or are fascinated with.
2. Make an oral history using audiotape or video.
3. Listen for the person's use of words, his or her delivery, the manner in which the story is being told.

MODERN POETRY: WILLIAMS, O'NEILL, AND MAMET

Tennessee Williams's Heroines

Amanda in *The Glass Menagerie,* Maggie in *Cat on a Hot Tin Roof,* Alma in *Summer and Smoke* are all poets/storytellers. They spin their biographies, their desires, their dreams with words that hold the audience in rapt attention. Blanche DuBois in *A Streetcar Named Desire* (we shouldn't forget that she's an ex-English teacher) uses language as a way of life: She can hide from reality, she can use her fantasies to lie to herself, she can defend herself, she can impress, cajole, charm, and breathe all because of words. Blanche can deny that she is a schoolteacher, a neurotic, a prostitute, an alcoholic. In her mind, she is an artist, an artist who paints with language. And she's right. For Blanche language is what sets her above the animals of this world. Language purges the darkness of her experience. Language transforms her.

Example
Even though we are taking it out of context, let's look at Blanche's
following speech. It is self-explanatory. She is talking to her sister,
Stella. Examine it for her use of images.

Blanche: I, I, I took the blows in my face and my body! All
those deaths! The long parade to the graveyard!
Father, mother! Margaret, that dreadful way! So big
with it, it couldn't be put in a coffin! But had to be
burned like rubbish! You just came home in time for
the funerals, Stella. And funerals are pretty compared
to deaths. Funerals are quiet, but deaths—not always.
Sometimes their breathing is hoarse, and sometimes
it rattles, and sometimes they even cry out to you,
Don't let me go! . . .

Exercise: Work the Images
inside Your Imagination

1. Being hit in your face and body. How hard? How much
   did it hurt you?
2. Seeing many people dying, an endless stream of coffins
   and automobiles and people to the graveyard
3. The "graveyard." Two syllables, very hard sounding
4. The family, the ones closest to you, dying
5. "So big with it, it couldn't be put in a coffin." People so
   bloated with disease that they couldn't fit into a coffin,
   they had to be burned
6. Your sister coming home after all the pain and suffering
   are over
7. Death as something specific, a nightmare
8. The living trying to breathe
9. The sound of the dying, the sound of the death rattle
10. The terror of dying
11. The desperation of not wanting to die

You can see how Blanche's language is a form of poetry. All these images reverberate. How do they affect you? The actress begins to see the images in her imagination. They'll take root there, and when it comes time to "act," you will have the distinct advantage of knowing what you are talking about. Better still, you will be seeing what you are talking about.

Exercise: The Need to Speak

Blanche has never told any of this to her sister. Her sister went away, got married, and did not have the burden of mother, father, relatives—of dealing with them and trying to hold things together. There seems to be an undercurrent of anger in the speech, some real resentment. Blanche is very poetic, but it's not poetry for its own sake. It is poetry that comes from wanting to express something very important. She has a profound need to speak. Find times in your own life when you had such a need.

1. Examine the times in your own life when you needed very much to speak. What happened? What did you say? What did it feel like as you said it? Do it again.
2. Examine when you said something that you had been holding back to a close relative. A confession, a piece of information, a long-standing resentment you finally got out. Can you recapture what it was like—having to get it off your chest?
3. Recall a time when you felt very wronged by what someone had done to you and you finally told that person so. What was it like to really tell someone off? Can you recapture those impulses?

Exercise: More of the Need to Speak

1. Observe someone who loves to tell stories.
2. Observe someone who is a compulsive talker.
3. Observe someone who likes to gossip.

You will find that their talking takes a great deal of energy. They take a particular pleasure in the act of talking. They use language in a very colorful way. They have some real need within them to speak. And they are encouraged by your listening.

Eugene O'Neill's Confessions

Long Day's Journey into Night is O'Neill's play about himself (Edmund), his brother Jamie, and his mother and father. It takes place in a twenty-four-hour period in their summer house in New London, Connecticut. The play is a tragedy, and it reveals a series of truths about each character. The following speech is Edmund talking to his father, James Tyrone. It is the last act of the play, both have been drinking whiskey. Edmund is a would-be writer (O'Neill himself, actually), and he suffers from TB and has to go to a sanitarium. As he and his father converse, his mother, Mary Tyrone (a morphine addict), is upstairs alone.

Edmund: (*Staring before him*) The fog was where I wanted to be. Halfway down the path you can't see this house. You'd never know it was here. Or any of the other places down the avenue. I couldn't see but a few feet ahead. I didn't meet a soul. Everything looked and sounded unreal. Nothing was what it is. That's what I wanted—to be alone with myself in another world where truth is untrue and life can hide from itself. Out beyond the harbor, where the road runs along the beach, I even lost the feeling of being on land. The fog and the sea seemed part of each other. It was like walking on the bottom of the sea. As if I had drowned long ago. As if I was a ghost belonging to the fog, and the fog was the ghost of the sea. It felt damned peaceful to be nothing more than a ghost within a ghost. . . .

Tyrone: (*Impressed and at the same time revolted*) You have a poet in you but it's a damned morbid one!

Exercise

Examine Edmund's speech for its images as you did Blanche's speech. The speech is out of context, but it is vivid enough to be worked independently. We are not adding emotion or intention to the speech. We just want to examine the language itself.

1. Try seeing the images, one at a time.
2. Slowly put the images together.
3. Do you see what Edmund saw?
4. Are you experiencing what he's saying?
5. Does just working the language let you into what he's describing?

The images should help you focus on the story Edmund is telling. As you work it notice:

1. Time
2. Place
3. Atmosphere and mood
4. Point of view
5. Events
6. Most importantly, *movement*

There is action that the character is observing and action that the character is doing. There is nothing static in the speech. As with Blanche's speech, with Edmund's there is a sense of the story moving forward. This is what makes the language dramatic.

David Mamet's Macho Men

You can tell a great deal about Blanche and Edmund from the way they speak. On the other hand, certain characters use speech to reveal not who they are but rather who they would like to be. Here's a character who fancies himself a great Romeo. He sits down at a table in a bar occupied by a woman whom he doesn't know and who hasn't invited him, and before you know it, this is coming out of his mouth:

> **Bernie:** . . . So here I am. I'm just in town for a one-day
> layover, and I happen to find myself in this bar. So,
> so far so good. What am I going to do? I could
> lounge alone and lonely and stare into my drink, or
> I could take the bull by the horns and make an effort
> to enjoy myself . . .
> . . . So hold on. So I see you seated at this table and
> I say to myself, "Doug McKenzie, there is a young
> woman," I say to myself, "What is she doing here?" and
> I think she is here for the same reasons as I. To enjoy
> herself, and perhaps, to meet provocative people.
> (*Pause*) I'm a meteorologist for TWA. It's an incredibly
> interesting, but lonely job. . . . Stuck in the cockpit of
> some jumbo jet hours at a time . . . nothing to look at
> but charts . . . what are you drinking?

It's quite a come-on!

Do you believe he's a meteorologist? Do you believe his name is Doug McKenzie? His name is Bernard Litko. He has a job in an office. The play is *Sexual Perversity in Chicago*. Bernard uses language to make himself interesting. He spins fantasies to such a degree that you wonder if he believes them himself. He's the white-collar poet of sexuality and sexism: He fancies himself a great ladies' man. However, Bernard uses language to do verbally what he can't do in actuality. He uses language as a substitute for experience. Later in this same scene he turns on this woman. Language becomes his weapon against rejection.

The "Without Emotion" Exercise

When actors get their hands on a speech they tend immediately to begin emoting all over the place. Half the time you can't follow the story because there is so much emotional drama being delivered. Variation, progression, change of topic, events all go out the window.

Take any of the three preceding speeches, or one from your own library, and try to work on it without emotion. Put yourself in a neutral space, that is, a frame of mind where you concentrate only on the words and keep all feeling, all emotion out.

Example: The *Sexual Perversity* Speech of Bernie

Close your eyes and see the images of:

1. In town
2. What to do?
3. Lounging alone and lonely
4. Staring into my drink
5. Taking the bull by the horns
6. An effort to enjoy myself

Keep it flat, just see it. Don't worry about the girl you are talking to, don't worry about being slow, about being boring, about being untheatrical. Let the words work themselves. Do not control them, do not impose any emotional life onto them. Try this four or five times. Go on to the second section of the speech. Try that as many times. Put the whole speech together.

Bernie has an agenda here: He's trying to pick up this girl. However, keep that out of the exercise. The point is this: If you see it, Bernie sees it. When he sees it, the girl sees it.

SHAKESPEARE: IMAGES AND VERBS

The following three lines are from Juliet's balcony scene, declaring her love to Romeo:

> *My bounty is as boundless as the sea,*
> *My love as deep; the more I give to thee,*
> *The more I have, for both are infinite.*

Imagine saying anything like that to someone you had met only a few hours before. As a matter of fact, you were both wearing masks.

You touched hands, though, and it all got kind of sexy because he was flirting. Now he's in your garden, and you're up on your balcony, and he shouldn't be there because his family and your family are enemies, but he has been saying all these crazy things about loving you and suddenly you find yourself confessing how much you love him, too.

Making Sense of the Words

The actor in you begins to work. You start by trying to understand Juliet's words.

What's *bounty*? That's the capacity for giving. How much capacity? *Boundless as the sea.*

What's the meaning of *boundless*? An amount so large it cannot be measured. So you have this enormous capacity for giving and loving. Not only that. The more love you have to give from this bounty, the more you have *for both are infinite!* These are the first three lines of a speech. Deal with them first by saying them aloud a few times.

Verb Exercise

Verbs are the glue that holds the narrative together. They define action, movement, and events and give the narrative its thrust. Without the verbs properly delivered, the audience does not have much chance to understand the speech. And if the verbs are not properly delivered, or if they are ignored, glossed over, muttered, or finessed, the actor doesn't really know what he's talking about.

Look at Juliet's three preceding lines: "My bounty is as boundless as the sea" and so on. Men *and* women, for the purposes of the exercise, can try it.

1. After you've tried saying the speech, look at the verbs in those three lines:
   is
   give
   have
   are

Very simple language. *Is, give, have, are.* Almost like: "something is"

"I *give*"
"these I *have*"
"which *are*"

2. Do the speech silently except that when you come to the verbs, say each one aloud. So that in your mind you're saying "My bounty," but when you come to the verb "is" you say that aloud. Continue the rest in your mind and say the next verb aloud, and so forth.

Keep doing that—*is, give, have,* and *are*—until you are ready to add any additional words aloud. But add slowly. You might now be saying aloud:

"*—bounty is—boundless*"
"*—love—give to thee*"
"*—I have—are infinite*"

Sensing the Images

The verb exercise will help make your feelings available so that you can experience the images.

1. *Bounty is boundless.* That's a very emotionally open feeling.
2. The word *love* is open in feeling; the confessing of the love is equally open. You feel like you want to shout it to the world—only you can't because it's night, people are asleep, and any relationship between you and a Montague is prohibited.
3. *Bounty* and *boundless* have the same open sound as the word *proud.* And essentially Juliet is displaying her love proudly.

Go back to the beginning each time. Repeat what you have done and slowly add a few more words:

—bounty is as boundless as—sea

Now you are into the image of the sea. And you might feel the need to pick up the word *deep* next.

My love as deep; the more I give to thee

Now your love and the sea are the same. *Boundless* and *deep*.

My bounty is as boundless as the sea,
My love as deep.

The images of the language will, hopefully, work on you so that after you see them you will have to say them. Or saying them will make you see them. They are one.

Juliet *is* the language, and the language is the character.

The feeling of the night, the mystery, the heat, the longing help create the language within her. It erupts from her feelings, which she wants to indulge in with long, legato sounds: *bounty, boundless, love, deep, infinite.*

ONE IMAGE AS AN IDEA THAT THE CHARACTER IMPROVISES ON

The Image of Light

Romeo, too, is no slouch when it comes to creating impromptu images of language. He's a poet himself. He loves words, women, and being in love. At the start of the balcony scene he finds himself inside Juliet's garden. He looks up at her house:

But soft! What light through yonder window breaks?
It is the East, and Juliet is the sun!
Arise, fair sun, and kill the envious moon,
Who is already sick and pale with grief
That thou her maid art far more fair than she . . . .

After you've done the work on the verbs and slowly built up the need to add the other words, you might find that you can use the different images of light to connect to the whole monologue. Light and love become one thing in Shakespeare's love poetry. Juliet is the sun, the fair sun. She is brighter than the moon, which is jealous of her light. Later in the speech Romeo has built this image of light and love into:

The brightness of her cheek would shame those stars
As daylight doth a lamp; her eyes in heaven
Would through the airy region stream so bright
That birds would sing and think it were not night.

The Image of Darkness

Later in the play, contrasting with the imagery of the love object as being light, Shakespeare shows how Juliet evokes darkness as a place to make love. She is impatiently awaiting Romeo.

Gallop apace you fiery-footed steeds,
Towards Phoebus' lodging! Such a wagoner
As Phaeton would whip you to the west
And bring in cloudy night immediately.

Again, we begin by looking up all the words we are unclear of. We see that "fiery-footed steeds" refers to the horses of Phoebus (Apollo), god of the sun. "Towards Phoebus' lodging" refers to a place that is below the horizon. "Wagoner" must be a charioteer. "Phaeton" is the son of the sun god, who has a history of mismanaging the horses. The sun rises from the east and sets in the west. And the setting sun is the beginning of night. Juliet is invoking night to be brought on as quickly as possible, because with it comes Romeo, making it a *love-performing night.*

Back to Verbs

Try the verbs in an exercise again. They are:

gallop
whip
bring

These are three very active commands. Four lines of text, twenty-six words, forty syllables, three powerful verbs. Just keep saying those verbs until you are ready to build the first four lines of the speech (in actuality you want to do this with the entire speech).

The Actor Starts Owning the Words

When you have finally caught the *need* to say every word aloud, chances are you are going to hear horses. Horses galloping, coming toward you:

> *gallop*
> *apace*
> *you*
> *fiery-*
> *footed*
> *steeds*

Your words make the sound of horses pulling down the sun, bringing you Romeo. Go through the entire speech and build it slowly from the verbs. You will find the following:

1. Poetry need not be "poetical," that is, spoken in a breathy and artificial manner, nor with a fake English accent. It will be coming from you.
2. As the language comes out of your own mouth, you will not be imposing anything. The text will make sense to you because you are not standing in the way of it. It will then make sense to the audience.
3. The speech tells a story. With twists and events. Juliet is a poet. She spins images and verbalizes every nuance of love. She is a masterful storyteller.
4. Keep working, holding on to the images of the speech:

> See them.
> Feel them.
> Taste them.
> Say them.
> Become them.

Exercise: Paraphrasing the Lines

Try saying the text in your own words. Shakespeare won't be offended. Do not use any of the original language. Say it in your own way, with your own expressions, your own slang, making it as modern as today. This exercise tests how well you understand the monologue or the scene and how you are relating or connecting to the situation.

The Opera Exercise

We've been through the verb exercises and how they give you the *need to speak* the words that are given to you. And how each word, slowly added, helps you find the images that the story is built on. And how this all pivots on words of action: verbs.

I often do something called "the opera exercise." It's not my own invention, and I can't remember where I first came across it, but it can be very helpful. Sing your text. The text can be classical or modern, it makes no difference. Sing it fully, openly, don't hold anything back. Don't worry if you can sing or not. Don't worry about sounding ridiculous. Sing it as though you were in the opera version of the play that is being performed at the Met. Interesting things will happen. You will paint the words in a very colorful way. You will be able to grab onto the words that are most dramatic and the words that need not be stressed at all. And mainly, you will find your breath. If you run out of breath before the line is over, you'll want to go back to the beginning of the line and retime it. In Shakespeare—even in the Williams and O'Neill pieces cited—the lines are often long, and if you mistime your breathing you will have no air left to finish the end of the line. In Shakespeare, the end of the line is the point! If you have chopped that off or dropped it breathlessly, your audience will neither hear it nor make sense of it. Much of acting is on the breath, and the opera exercise helps you build up your breath as your inner ear targets which sound to land on next.

After you've done this exercise several times, go back to the speech and do it "straight." Then, go back and do the opera version again. See how much of a difference there is. Keep working back and forth until you think you've created a fusion of the two, that is, you are in character, but your breath, timing, and delivery of the text are what you did in the opera.

■ ‖ ■ ‖ ■ ‖ ■ ‖ ■ ‖ ■ ‖ ■ ‖ ■ ‖ ■ ‖ ■ ‖ ■ ‖ ■ ‖ ■ ‖ ■ ‖ ■ ‖ ■

FREQUENTLY ASKED QUESTIONS

Q: Can the opera exercise, paraphrasing, and the verb exercises be done as effectively with modern pieces as classical material?

A: Very much so.

Q: There seems to be a trick that the actor has to go between playing a character who speaks in elevated or poetic language and being a real person. Is this true?

A: Absolutely.

1. As beautiful as language can be, it is a terrible trap for actors to intone, get tremulous, and let the audience know they are being poetical. Actors eventually understand that "poetry" is second nature to the character. It comes out of the character's mouth freely and unselfconsciously. For example, the Tyrone family is of Irish descent. The gift of gab—the gift of the spoken word—is in their genes. They are literate: They know poetry and Shakespeare and toss imagery around the house with abandon. The father and the older brother are actors. Language is their bread and butter. And Edmund, representing the young O'Neill, is a budding writer. They like to speak, they want to speak, they have to speak. The language they speak is their reality and should be a great tool for the actor when it comes time to play any of them.

2. The other trap that actors sometimes fall into: deliberately not being poetic; hence they "naturalize" the

language. This means they make everything sound like what they think real folk sound like. But this is as artificial as rhapsodizing the text.

The more the actor naturalizes the language, the harder it is to hear because the sentences become garbled, the ends of lines are chopped off, one thought does not progress from the one that preceded it. The audience can't follow it.

Q: Previously you talked about acting as performing and how the actor shouldn't just experience things for his own benefit and about not "getting it out there." But in this chapter you talk about being neutral, which seems a contradiction.

A: It is. When you are working with textual images you want to start from a very private base. You are communing between yourself and the author. The work needs to be done for you and you alone. Much of the actor's process is like this. However, there is always another step. If you are truly seeing the images, you will be performing them. You will be performing them very simply and truthfully. They will be coming from within you and out of your mouth as though you owned the words.

On the one hand, you don't want to push the images into a fake, air-filled, and clichéd performance; on the other, you don't want to keep the images to yourself forever.

If the images are seen by you, they will be screaming to get out. You will want to let them. They'll almost do it themselves if you've done the work I'm talking about.

Q: When you talk about documenting people, how about documenting myself? I have a tape recorder and would like to play back what I'm working on or even my own stories. What do you think?

continued on page 64

continued from page 63

A: I think listening to oneself is like acting in front of the mirror. It's fundamentally a very dead way of working. Actors who work in front of the mirror focus on what they remember they looked like and try to replicate the memory. Nothing is lived on stage. You really mustn't appear to be looking at yourself, or listening to yourself.

However, here's another contradiction. (And by the way, art, like life, is full of them.) Try it. It may work for you. But be aware of mechanical acting.

Q: What about listening to performances of plays?

A: If it's a play you're in, I'd worry about that. The performance might be very indelible and make it hard for you to invent your own. But if it's material you are not immediately working on, yes. As a student of an art form, you want to be its historian as well.

Q: I really need to keep my voice and speech work up, building my voice as an interesting instrument, developing breath support, resonance, and articulation. All the while doing work on text for images, verbs, and story?

A: That's right. Your vocal skills will illuminate the meaning of the text as much as a dancer's body illuminates the choreography.

Q: What's next?

A: We are taking the facts of the story, our awareness of language, to enter the text subjectively.

Q: What does that mean?

A: It's the beginning of making choices to act the material.

6

|| ■ || ■ || ■ ||

READING THE TEXT (SUBJECTIVELY)

You've examined the text as objectively as possible for the time being, knowing that this is just the beginning of your getting to know the material. Now comes the time when you just want to dig in and deal with your role. You want to start finding out what makes your character tick. The process of interpreting your role begins. Now you are reading the play with an eye to examining specifics about your character. The process becomes very subjective at this point because you are visualizing your character's behavior and you are visualizing yourself playing that character on the stage.

When you read the play subjectively you begin to interpret the play in acting terms. The objective reading has shown you the facts of the play. But now you are looking for implications, nuances, truths that are buried between the lines in an effort to come to certain insights about the character. The insights that the actor collects in reading are the ones that are tried in rehearsal. The ones that work invariably stay in the show. The ones that do not work evolve into ones that do.

ARTICULATING YOUR INSTINCTS ABOUT WHAT YOU ARE READING

By now you have a great many feelings about and responses to what you are reading. You need to go with them. Articulate what you are feeling about your character. Get to the areas that you can't quite articulate but you have a strong instinct about. Try verbalizing those areas somehow.

Sketch Out Your Character's Story

Exercise

Tell the story of your character as it happens in the course of the play. "I am the prince of Denmark. I live in a castle at Elsinore. It is the *year*—." Tell the story to yourself. See if you get it straight. Write it down. As you write it, feel free to add any interpretation that comes to mind. For example, "Of course, this closet scene with Hamlet and his mother is completely sexual." You can play armchair detective or supershrink all over the place. Get all your ideas out on paper. You don't have to be concerned about being wrong because no one except you is going to read this.

It might be helpful to say "I" do such and such rather than "he" does such and such because you want to start a process of becoming your character. Skip nothing. There will be times when your character is offstage. Fill in the offstage story. Later, this will be discussed as a specific technique, but for now, sketch it out.

Exercise

Tell your character's physical story. Eliminate the dialogue given to your character and, without it, see if there is a physical story that is being told. The story of Blanche in Williams's *A Streetcar Named Desire* is as strong physically as it is verbally. Blanche comes to New Orleans to visit her sister for the first time. The atmosphere is alien to her because she thinks her sister has "lowered" herself socially by living in such a place. Imagine Blanche's movement through this atmosphere. Imagine her as she got off the streetcar named Desire and walked to this place on a hot day. Her body craves alcohol, her nerves are unsteady, she needs a hot bath, a long hot bath. Write about all the other physical things that happen to her in the story. After Stanley enters, it's all physical. Her emotional deterioration manifests itself not only as delusions, but physically as well. As you work on the role you will find a very complete physical picture.

Figure Out What Your Character Wants

Exercise
At first it may seem that your character wants quite a few things. Make a list. Don't worry how long it is. For example:

> Hamlet wants to avenge his father's murder.
> He wants to make up his mind.
> He wants to avoid murder.
> He wants to sleep with Gertrude.

No matter how farfetched or way out, go with your instincts and enjoy the process because you will find that most of the things you come up with eventually will be of use.

Exercise
Write a very short explanation of what justifies your character's wants. Why does Hamlet want to avoid making certain decisions? Why does he want to avenge his father? Why does Blanche want a drink? Why does she want to visit her sister? Keeping the reason, the justification, or the explanation of what motivates your character's wants very short will help you get to the crux of the matter. On the one hand you want to feel free to write what is on your mind, but on the other hand you don't have to feel obliged to write a long, intellectual essay. You want your instincts to flow. You don't have to get bogged down with how clever you are by complicating things.

Look for the Obstacles That Stand in the Way of What Your Character Wants

In any story there are obstacles or roadblocks that make it difficult for a character to achieve what is wanted. These obstacles make the pursuit more interesting for the audience to watch. The audience wants to see how your character is going to overcome these obstacles. Obstacles come in various sizes and shapes and occur with great regularity during the course of a play. Examples are:

1. **A physical obstacle:** You are an astronaut who wants to explore the moon, but during your mission there is a problem with your spaceship. This problem is an obstacle. In this case, the obstacle causes you to change what you want. You just want to get safely home.

   There are stories in which physical obstacles such as the preceding one will change what a character wants. More likely they will challenge your character to intensify the want: Climbing a mountain, crossing a river, "come hell or high water" you are going to get what you are after.

2. **A psychological obstacle:** If you are playing Blanche in *A Streetcar Named Desire*, your brother-in-law, Stanley Kowalski, is certainly a physical obstacle for you, but he is also a psychological one. You want to get away with your lies and your illusions. He will not let you. He is someone who is always in the way of what you want, and you have to work your way around him.

3. **An emotional obstacle:** Hamlet's inaction becomes an obstacle to himself. He lacerates himself with self-loathing and despair, which weaken him into further inaction. His own feelings about himself and his moral dilemma are obstacles to what he wants. In other cases, a strong emotion such as fear can be an obstacle: fear of dying, fear of taking a risk, fear of loss.

4. **External obstacles:** A sick parent whom you cannot leave, a lack of money that prevents you from getting what you want, a feud between families that prevents you from pursuing a love object, different religions, opposing ideologies, social mores, and so on are all recurrent obstacles in plays.

Sometimes the obstacles create one hurdle after another that the character must overcome. Among the many hurdles that Romeo has to get over in the balcony scene of *Romeo and Juliet* are the distance between him and his loved one; his being a Montague and her being a Capulet, which makes them children of sworn enemies; the night that assists in hiding the couple but also makes the threat of discovery dangerous; and, most crucial, Juliet's uncertainty about Romeo's seriousness.

Exercise

Write down all the obstacles that get in your character's way. Make sure that the following things are becoming clear to you in terms of your character:

1. Your character's story
2. Your character's wants
3. The things that stand in the way of achieving those wants

FINDING WHAT'S ACTABLE

It's possible for a character to want many things at one time, or to want conflicting things, or not even to know what he or she wants. It all depends on the play. Generally, however, your character will want one or two things very strongly and will spend every instant of stage time trying to get those things.

When exploring Romeo in the balcony scene you may have written:

I want to be a lover.
I want to dazzle her with my poetry.
I want to live dangerously.
I want to woo the socks off her.
I want to let her know I'm a fun guy.
I want her to vow to be mine.
I want her to let me come up.
I want her to come down here.
I want to make love to her.

All these wants and many more are possible. But which does the actor play and how? Can the actor convey all these wants in one scene? How do you sort them out?

FINDING "THE OBJECTIVES" THAT ARE THE STRONGEST

Your objective is what your character is pursuing in the course of the play. It's really what you most deeply want as a character. Objectives are large and usually hard to attain. The audience sits in its seats because it wants to see you attain your objective, such as walking on the moon, or see you not attain it, such as murdering an innocent person.

An objective is strongest when it can be simply stated and passionately pursued. If you are doing a play in which your character goes through complicated maneuvers to become the king of England, at least you know you have a very simple, strong objective that gets you through the play: "I want to be king." The actor should always be able to state the objective very clearly. Looking at Romeo's list of wants you might say that the clearest, simplest, strongest objective he has in the balcony scene is: "I want to make love to Juliet."

Test Your Choice of Objective against the Following to See How Strong It Is

1. What you want must be attained. There can be no two ways about it. The appetites and desires of your character must be full to the brim. An objective without a passionate need for attainment will prove to be weak. You must attain it; you *will* attain it.

Outside forces often press on the character to attain the objectives.

2. Something must be at stake or of a certain magnitude to generate the want. In *Romeo and Juliet*, the life force

that kindles the characters' love for each other is irre-
pressible. Life, death, survival, and happiness are some
of the conditions that give an objective impetus.
3. Your want requires immediate fulfillment. Richard III
has waited long enough. He is going to get the crown of
England now. As a matter of fact, the first word in the
play is "Now." After Juliet decides she wants Romeo, she
can barely wait until the "morrow" for consummation.

The old question of "how is this night different from all
others?" is answered by the fact that your character is on the stage,
pursuing an objective in the present tense. Now. Immediately. It
cannot wait.

4. Your wants are selfishly sought. Romeo is not pursuing
Juliet for the good of mankind. He wants her for his own
fulfillment.

Romeo is pursuing his own need for happiness. Young actors
often have a problem with this. They want to make "soft" choices
so they can be liked. You have to advocate your character's cause,
no matter what it makes you look like. Nice guys usually aren't
interesting characters. Your character is driven by what he or
she wants. Yes, there are characters who are subtle, sophisticated, caring, and delicate, but they are still, in their own indirect
way, driven as stageworthy beings who are part of a dramatic story.

Take a Subjective Reading of Your Own Life and Try These Exercises

1. Keep a Journal
Think of your life as more dramatic than it actually is (if you don't
do so already). Write about what happened to you yesterday.
It could be called "A Day in the Life of (Yourself)."

Put down the highlights.
What were some of the things you wanted?

What do you always want lately?
What are the obstacles to your getting what you
    really want?
Who gets in your way?
Will you ever get what you want?

2. Observation: Look at the World around You

Study people you know very well. What do they want?
How do they overcome their obstacles?
Study children to see how many things they want all the time.
    How do they get what they want?

THE THINGS THAT YOU ARE DOING TO GET WHAT YOU WANT ARE YOUR ACTIONS

Finding Actions to Play

Objectives are achieved through actions. Actions are what the actor plays. This is a very simple concept, yet it gives many actors trouble and takes years to master. It's like saying, "There's the piano and here's the music for Beethoven's *Moonlight Sonata.* Sit down and play it." It will probably take you a while. Actions are the line-by-line, very active, very specific things your character is doing. Actions may be very direct, or quite indirect, which we will explore during the course of this book. Actions are what give your character interest.

Going back to Romeo and the list of his wants, you can now see that the strongest choice that meets our criteria for an objective is "I want to make love to her." It is now possible to see that the other wants on that list are very playable actions to get that one objective. They are what your character is doing to get what he wants. They are the active means he employs to win Juliet:

Dazzling her with my gift for language
Making her want to listen to me all night because I'm
 so special
Showing her how courageous I am
Inviting her to come down
Inviting myself to come up
Flattering her for the thrill of it
Making her laugh
Making her feel beautiful, special, wonderful
Trying to exchange vows, and so on

Exercises

With a partner, improvise the following:

1. A Direct Approach

    a. *One objective, one action: You* want to borrow money from a friend. Try one action, such as begging, and see where that gets you.

    b. *Two actions, one objective: You* want the money. You try begging for it. It fails. You con the other person into thinking it's going to be good for him or her to lend you the money.

    c. *Three actions:* After you have tried the first two, see if this works: You intimidate the person into making the loan.

2. An Indirect Approach

You need money desperately. You want to get it from a friend. You cannot ask directly. How do you play this scene? What would your actions be? Perhaps you want your friend to come up with the idea of lending you the money and making you take it. Your action is almost the reverse of your objective: "Oh, no, I couldn't accept the money" on the outside while secretly you are saying, "Give me more."

Further Work on Actions

Let's explore the opening moments of Ibsen's *A Doll's House* to further illuminate the idea of actions.

The play opens with Nora coming home with parcels and letting in a porter who carries a Christmas tree and a basket, which he gives to the maid.

Nora: Hide the Christmas tree, carefully, Helen. Be sure the children do not see it till this evening, when it is dressed. (*To the Porter; taking out her purse*) How much?

Porter: Sixpence.

Nora: There is a shilling. No, keep the change. (*The Porter leaves and Nora shuts the door. She takes a bag of macaroons from her pocket and eats one or two; then goes cautiously to her husband's door and listens.*) Yes, he is in.

Helmer: (*Calls from his room*) Is that my little lark twittering out there?

Nora: (*Busy opening some of the parcels*) Yes, it is!

Helmer: Is my little squirrel bustling about?

Nora: Yes!

Helmer: When did my little squirrel come home?

Nora: Just now. (*Puts the bag of macaroons into her pocket and wipes her mouth*) Come in here, Torvald, and see what I have bought.

Helmer: Don't disturb me. (*A little later, he opens the door and looks into the room, pen in hand.*) Has my little spendthrift been wasting money again?

Nora: Yes, but, Torvald, this year we really can let ourselves go a little. This is the first Christmas that we have not needed to economize.

Helmer: Still, you know, we can't spend money recklessly.

Nora: Yes, Torvald, we may be a wee bit reckless now, mayn't we? Just a tiny wee bit! You are going to have a big salary and earn lots and lots of money.

Helmer: Yes, after the New Year; but then it will be a whole quarter before the salary is due.
Nora: Pooh! We can borrow till then.

Nora's objective here is to make everyone happy at Christmas because there is so much to celebrate. Nora's actions are fairly direct. They are:

Hiding the Christmas tree from her children
Giving the porter a generous tip
Sneaking a few macaroons that she's not supposed to eat
Opening what she has purchased to show her husband

Her husband, Helmer, enters, and she wants to share her Christmas purchases with him. Her actions are:

Greeting her husband
Hiding the macaroons

He is upset and worried about money. Nora wants to avoid an argument. Her actions become more indirect as she deals with him. In order to avoid conflict and to get him into the Christmas spirit, her actions are:

Charming him
Reassuring him that there is nothing to worry about
Making light of their debts

These are very actable choices all connected to a main objective. After Helmer enters, Nora's actions are tempered by the fact that he is the obstacle to what she wants. She literally "plays" around him to get what she wants.

Exercise
I call this the "I want" exercise. It really should be called the "I want to do" exercise because it is designed to give you the impetus not only to do, but also to positively want to do what you are doing! It will get you to roughly the same place as did our

preceding analysis, but it might result in some richer choices. The goal here is to get the actor to feel the impulse for action, then to verbalize it.

As Nora, before you've said the line Ibsen has given you, listen intently to what the other character has just said to you. What has been said will kick off an emotional or intellectual response from you. Verbalize that response by prefacing it with "I want."

Helmer: (*Calls from his room*) Is that my little lark twittering out there?

  Nora: (*Busy opening some of the parcels*) "*I want to surprise him with these lovely things.*" Yes, it is!

Helmer: Is my little squirrel bustling about?

  Nora: "*I want to finish this macaroon fast.*" Yes!

Helmer: When did my little squirrel come home?

  Nora: "*I want to give myself a few more seconds.*" Just now. "*I want to hide these sweets.*" (*Puts the bag of macaroons into her pocket and wipes her mouth*) "*I want him to like everything.*" Come in here, Torvald, and see what I have bought.

Helmer: Don't disturb me. (*A little later, he opens the door and looks into the room, pen in hand.*) Has my little spendthrift been wasting money again?

  Nora: "*I want him to forget money for once.*" Yes, but, Torvald, this year we really can let ourselves go a little. "*I want him to be as happy as I am.*" This is the first Christmas that we have not needed to economize.

And so forth. The italicized lines in quotation marks are the possible improvised responses that Nora has to Helmer. (I say "possible" because these are my choices, and you have to feel free to find your own.)

The exercise helps you connect to something you really want to do on each of the written lines. It gives you something spe-cific to play, moment to moment. Hence, it's not just a question of academically listing your actions and routinely trotting them out. Your character has to really want to do each and every one of them.

Exercise: "She Wants/I Want"
Among other advantages of this exercise, it tests your skills in listening to the other actor, as well as your concentration. Listen to what the other character is saying to you and out loud improvise, "She wants—." And as a result of your thinking that you know what she wants, you then say, "I want—" and add in the written line. As Helmer, your objective is to try to control Nora. You love her, but she's delightfully childish and a spendthrift. You call her "little squirrel" because she is always bringing things home and hiding them from you. You enter and see all the purchases:

Helmer: *"She wants to bankrupt me. I want to stop her."* Has my little spendthrift been wasting money again?

Nora tells you that "This is the first Christmas that we have not needed to economize."

Helmer: *"She wants me to have a good time. I want her to have fun, but within reason."* Still, you know, we can't spend money recklessly.

Nora tells Helmer about his raise, that soon he will "earn lots and lots of money."

Helmer: *"She wants to spend money that's not there. I want to show her some reality."* Yes, after the New Year; but then it will be a whole quarter before the salary is due.

Now that you are aware of this concept, study performances on stage and on film to see how the actors are handling their objectives and playing their actions.

■ || ■ || ■ || ■ || ■ || ■ || ■ || ■ || ■ || ■ || ■ || ■ || ■ || ■ || ■ || ■

FREQUENTLY ASKED QUESTIONS

Q: By a "subjective reading of the text" you mean that I, the actor, can fully use my imagination to visualize my character through the course of the play?

A: That's correct.

Q: But what if I go astray? What if I begin to imagine things that the author did not intend?

A: Don't edit your imagination! Never do that. The author will be flattered that he or she has created something that vivid in your head. Later, you will make choices. But at the start open yourself to experiencing your own instincts.

Q: As I tell my character's story, are there any special tips you can give?

A: Ask the following questions:
1. Does your character grow or remain the same?
2. Does your character learn anything?
3. What happened that made your character change?

Q: What if I choose the wrong objective?

A: Life is not a blue book. There is no right, no wrong in an artistic process; there is just getting on with it. If what you have chosen as an objective does not work, try something else.

Q: Do you always know what your objective is?

A: Sometimes you just jump right in and hope you'll find out what your character is really after, because it is not clear to you. Until you find your objective or objectives you are basically running on empty: If your character is not pursuing something very actively, he or she does not belong in the play.

Q: Can you have more than one objective?

A: Your character can have more than one objective. There can be contrasting objectives, as will be explored with Trepleff in *The Sea Gull*. But the actor can play only one thing at a time.

Q: Do you ever change objectives in the course of the play?

A: Yes, the objective can change in the course of a play. Nora in *A Doll's House* certainly does not start out wanting to leave her husband and children. But when an objective changes, it is usually not inconsistent with all that has gone before it. It may reverse a whole pattern, but it doesn't come from out of the blue.

Q: Do you recommend "marking" your script, that is, breaking the text down into actions and objectives and writing it all down?

A: Marking your script has these advantages:

1. You can see how the text was built and how specific you have to be. It keeps you from being general.
2. You can see the progression of your character clearly.
3. You can locate patterns of behavior quickly.
4. And if you are a student, the play is something you get back to, not something you do exclusively all day long. Therefore, your notations are refreshers when you return to them.

There are traps, however. Here's an example of one:

I was working with a student on a scene and asked at a certain point what he was playing on a particular line. He said that he had forgotten but

continued on page 80

continued from page 79

that it was right there in his book. He asked to
look up what he had written down.

You have to play what is happening between you
and the other actor. You can't be concentrating on
trying to remember how you marked your script.
Acting has to be how people on the stage make
something happen together, in the same moment.

Q: I feel that when you talk about actions and objectives
you like choices that make the character very aggressive. Is that true?

A: Your question suggests to me that you are a kind person who does not like conflict. Is that true?

Q: Yes. Why?

A: Your character will always be involved in dramatic
conflict.

Q: What do you mean by "conflict"?

A: *Conflict* is variously defined as:
1. to be contradictory
2. in opposition; to clash; to disagree
3. fight, battle, or struggle
4. antagonism or opposition, as between interests or
   principles
5. discord of action, feeling, or effect
6. incompatibility of idea, event, or activity with another
7. opposing demands or interests

Conflict in terms of argument, debate, friction, or
warfare is what energizes any play.
1. Characters wanting different things create conflict.
2. Characters wanting the same things but encoun-
   tering obstacles along the way create conflict.

Remember: In any good story the characters either
are in trouble or are trying to work themselves out of
a problem.

Q: Then that must be why a strong, playable objective has to have these conditions:
1. It must be attained.
2. Something has to be at stake.
3. Immediate fulfillment is necessary.
4. It is selfishly sought.

A: I couldn't have said it better myself.

PART II

THE PROCESS

A process that connects personal autobiography and improvising the text to the life of the character:

- The actor's imagination as it bridges self to character and character back to self

- Finding the most playable "I want"

THE IMAGINATIVE PROCESS (1)

Lee Strasberg believed that the actor should use emotions recalled from his own life as substitutions for the character's emotions. Stella Adler believed that that method was nonsense because Konstantin Stanislavski told her personally he disavowed any such idea, and that the actor had to use his or her imagination instead.

Who is right?

They are both right, and they are both wrong, because the actor really ends up using a combination of both autobiography and imagination. In many ways artists experience their imaginations far more intensely, live in their imaginations far more successfully than they do in the "real" world. This may be why some actors feel they do better in roles that they do not "relate" to. Other actors won't go near a role they have no connection to.

In any case, the actor makes a journey from himself into the play and back into himself again. This trip from self to text and back to self culminates as the character the audience sees on stage or on the screen.

But how exactly does this happen? What is the process? Reading has been stressed in earlier chapters. Understanding the author's intentions, how the play is built, and how the author uses language have been shown as tools that the actor must acquire. All that is the literal part of the work.

Not negating any of this, but instead complementing it, are ways of working that are nonliteral—ways of working that free the actor's imagination to find the bridge between self and text, between what the character is experiencing and how the actor can relate to it, or between what the actor has experienced and how that can be used as the character.

IMPROVISING AROUND THE TEXT

It's surprising how many actors don't want to improvise. They say, "Oh, I don't want to do that; let's just do the scene." What they mean by "doing the scene" is saying the lines and "acting." In defense of the actor who hates to improvise, I will say there are actors who are superb in an improv and are never very good in the actual scene. However, improvisation builds the actor's powers of imagination, and imagination is a muscle that always needs to be fed, developed, and put to use in the work.

What Improvisation Is

As we experienced in our work on the Basics, improvisation is anything the actor does that is not scripted. In much the same way a musician plays jazz, the actor can take a suggestion from the writing, such as a theme or an idea, and go wherever inspiration leads him. What happens is of the moment and can never happen again, at least not in the same way. If it's repeated, it is no longer an improvisation. In life we improvise all day long with conversations we've never had before, events that are new, and a script that has not been written down.

What Improvisation Does

Improvisation frees you from the author's lines and the obligation to "act." Improvisation gives you an opportunity to explore the world of the character, the world of the play, as well as your own imagination, reactions, and spontaneity.

How It's Done

John Guare's *Bosoms and Neglect* is not a very popular play, but it provides interesting and rewarding roles for an actor and an actress. It poses problems typical of many modern plays; it has a thread of universality that many of us have experienced, but it also has areas that some of us may not have experienced and may not be able to immediately relate to.

Background

The male character is Scooper; the female is Deirdre. The play takes place on the first day of August, when all the psychiatrists in New York City take off for vacation. Scooper and Deirdre happen to go to the same psychiatrist, Dr. James, and sometimes bump into each other in the waiting room. On this very hot morning, after each has had a last session until September, they coincidentally end up in Rizzoli's bookstore. They have never spoken to each other. She's at loose ends not knowing how to spend the rest of the day. His mother is in the hospital, being operated on for breast cancer. He and his best friend's wife are planning to run off to Haiti together that night.

Deirdre, who lives right across the street from Dr. James, invites Scooper to her apartment for a cool glass of wine. He accepts. Deirdre's apartment is filled with hundreds of books. Scooper and Deirdre have the following in common: a great love of books; Dr. James; anxiety about being separated from him for a month; and a sexual attraction to each other.

When the scene opens Scooper is describing in great detail his mother's cancer. Deirdre is listening intently.

Scooper: Imagine a peach that had an enormous bite taken out of it.
Deirdre: Oh, Christ.
Scooper: I'm not finished. Then. Then.
Deirdre: Calm.
Scooper: Was left in the back of a disconnected refrigerator for the winter months and you come back in the spring and open the icebox door and find the peach rotted where the bite was taken out. This poison gauze. This penicillin rot-mold. You could put your fist into the hole in her breast. The cancer was that deep.
Deirdre: Wait.
Scooper: She stood there, her blouse off. It's not so bad, she keeps saying. It is not so bad.

Deirdre: It's impossible. What you're describing.

Scooper: I saw it.

Deirdre: Cancer works slowly.

Scooper: I am telling you—I can't believe you are not believing me. I pour this out and your response is . . .

Deirdre: I'm not saying you're hallucinating. I'm saying cancer works inside, silently. Not like some horror show in a drive-in.

Scooper: She had so neglected herself that the disease was sick of not being noticed. The disease finally burst through her skin. The ulceration was like this screaming flesh, this breast screaming how loud do you have to go to get noticed?

Deirdre: Oh, Christ.

Scooper: The good part about being that old the metabolism moves so slowly that the cancer takes just that much longer.

Deirdre: And she had no medical aid?

Scooper: Sure. For two years, she's been laying Kotex over the wound, waving this tan plastic statue of Saint Jude, Patron of Lost Causes, over this small, expanding cavity in her chest, standing all night in the dark privacy of her open window so the midnight air would dry it out.

Deirdre: You never noticed?

Scooper: I never saw her.

Deirdre: In two years?

Scooper: She only likes talking on the phone. I can't see her. She can't see me. Gives her equal footing.

Deirdre: But her bladder . . .

Scooper: It was her uterus.

Deirdre: Oh, dear God.

Scooper: It fell out.

Deirdre: Oh no.

Scooper: Eighty-three-year-old muscles give out.

Deirdre: But still . . .

Scooper: The doctor who made the house call said this woman is finished. This woman will not make it through the day.

> "It's not so bad. Girl who cried wolf. False alarm." I paid
> off the doctor. Got Doctor James on the phone. Got her
> up to Columbia-Presbyterian.
>
> **Deirdre:** The best.
> **Scooper:** Doctor James waiting right there. He had a bed waiting,
> the best surgeon all lined up to see her.
> **Deirdre:** That was yesterday?
> **Scooper:** That was yesterday.
> **Deirdre:** And today she's on the table?
> **Scooper:** Right now.
> **Deirdre:** It makes me feel so well taken care of, like a fringe
> benefit, if anything happened to me.
> **Scooper:** Thanks to Doctor James.

The following are exercises that will help the actor connect to the character's life. Each exercise is in the form of an improvisation. These improvs are suggested, but after the actors get the hang of the work, they will be creating many of their own.

The process should be to do one or two improvs and then go into the scene. See how the experience and knowledge you are amassing from these exercises will help you in playing the scene.

> Dr. James's waiting room; encountering each other
> A session with the doctor that day, your last until September
> Meeting in Rizzoli's bookstore
> Work on the heat of the day
> Deirdre's apartment
> Love of books
> Deirdre's need for a relationship
> Scooper's connection to his mother

Exercise 1: Dr. James's Office

Either the actors have been in therapy or they have not. If they have had that experience, so much the better. If not, they are going to have to investigate this topic. What kind of doctor is Dr. James? A psychiatrist, psychologist, social worker? What's his methodology? Does the patient sit or lie on a couch? Is the doctor a Freudian? If so, what does that mean? What does each actor imagine him to look like? It's not necessary that they come up with the same answer because each has a different visual picture. The actors should agree on what Dr. James's office looks like and on what his waiting room looks like.

A Possible Improv

Each actor could take a turn arriving a bit early to see the doctor because there is something very specific that needs to be talked about.

> Find out if you can overhear the other person's session.
> Find out what happens when one leaves the doctor and meets the other in the waiting room. What would be said? Anything?
> Find out if you two are attracted to each other.
> Find out if you two look forward to bumping into each other there.

Exercise 2: A Session with the Doctor

A young woman I know was working on this scene and wanted to know what a therapy session was. She visited a doctor and has been going regularly now for two years. Find out what all this therapy business is about. If you don't want to go, read up on it, talk to people who have gone, or interview some doctors.

Improv

Set up a scene in which you are in the doctor's office. You have X amount of time to talk. Don't worry about what the doctor says; play that he just listens to you. Or choose an actor from the group to play Dr. James.

If you are playing Deirdre, deal with your feelings about Scooper: You don't know his name; he attracts you; you know you shouldn't ask, but what does the doctor think about this man? Or perhaps this man ignores you every time you see him. You dress for him, wear special perfume for him, and it irritates you no end that he just doesn't know you exist.

Scooper might talk about his mother, the woman in the waiting room (Deirdre), or the woman he is about to run away to Haiti with.
Make this session the last time you will see Dr. James for one month. You want to get it all in.
You need to say so much; you say very little.
Deal with your anxieties about separation from Dr. James.
Deal with your fears.

Don't script it in the sense that you know what you will say. Improvise on wherever your feelings take you.

Exercise 3: Meeting in Rizzoli's Bookstore

Both actors have to find out what this is all about. If you live in a city that has a Rizzoli's, it's easily explored. If there is none in your town, you have to find an equivalent. It's a store that sells art books, foreign magazines, foreign editions of certain books, and CDs. It's distinctive because it is very upscale in tone, usually very quiet, and perhaps for certain people, it is a place to browse, prowl, and cruise. Chances are if you meet someone there, he or she will be well read and well heeled. The store is always very beautiful, and you feel good being there. If your city does not have a Rizzoli's, you might imagine what it would be like if a store you know in your own city gave you that sense of well-being.

Improv
Both actors should go to the store and browse. See what happens. Then, do a scene in class based on the particulars of the store. Don't do what you did in the store, because repeating something is no longer improvising it. Bring your knowledge of the place into a situation in which Deirdre and Scooper see each other and have a great desire to connect. That's all! Let whatever happens happen.
Magazines such as *Paris Match* and *Oggi* are mentioned in the text as part of Rizzoli's. What are those magazines? Who's in them? Who do you think reads them? Use them in your improv and see if they help you get started with each other.

Exercise 4: Work on the Heat of the Day

This is one experience that the actors are bound to have had. Yet one of the hallmarks of student productions is how sensory work is disregarded. Actors play the same whether they are on top of Mount Everest or in the Mojave Desert.

Scooper might be dressed for travel, that is, he could be wearing a seersucker suit and a tie. He has books in his pocket and is carrying a suitcase. He's planning to go off to Haiti. It must be one hundred degrees in New York City, and it's only 10 A.M. Deirdre manages to seem cool, but is she? What is she wearing?

Improv
Each actor should explore walking along the pavement on a boiling day. Look for cool. How cool is Rizzoli's? How cool is the hallway of Deirdre's building? The elevator? Her apartment?

> Work on being in the heat and on how it increases your anxieties. You have problems, it is brutally hot, and you are about to explode.
> Recall what it's like to take your sweating body into an overly air-conditioned place. Are you chilled? Do you start to shake? How does your body work?
> Work on the extremes: the languorous rhythm that your body takes on when it is outdoors, the way your inner rhythms alter in air conditioning.

Exercise 5: Deirdre's Apartment

You must make this very specific. All too often the actors decide that "I'll sit here, and you sit there . . . and, oh, we'll have a few books," and that's it. Characters usually do not function in an unobserved world. I would like to think that the actors have taken great care in imagining the building that Deirdre lives in, both externally and internally. You obviously cannot bring in tons of objects for the scene, but it has to be worked out in your mind's eye.

> Draw a floor plan of her apartment.
> Discuss the type of decor and the way it makes each of you feel.
> Is there carpeting or wood floors? Tile floors? Art objects? Is it minimalist or cluttered? Did Deirdre decorate it herself? And for what purpose?
> What economic class does she belong to? Is she pretentious or modest in her taste?
> Has she ever had a man there?

Exercise 6: Love of Books

You always want to find the glue that binds the characters together in a scene. Both characters here are bibliophiles. They collect, read, and practically live inside books. Deirdre's apartment is full of books. I once worked on this scene when the young woman playing Deirdre had read nothing. I asked her how it was possible for her to reach her senior year at a major university having never read a book. She said she read only what was necessary to pass her courses. She asked if it was necessary to read all the books cited in the text. I told her it wouldn't hurt. She pointed out that there wasn't enough time.

She said she loved reading magazines "like *Vogue,* things like that. . . ." She asked what she should do.

One day before the scene began she told us stories about how her mother used to read to her as a child and how comforting all that was. We had no idea if this was the actress or the character as she imagined it. She talked about the healing nature of books and about how one could escape the real world and find understanding with what a fictional person is going through. It was completely convincing. I suppose that she combined the sense of what the character believed and a sense of where she intuited the teacher wanted her to go. Her talk to us worked positively for her, and she located where her character was coming from as far as her need for books was concerned.

Exercise 7: Deirdre's Need for a Relationship

Deirdre wants this man in her apartment. She wants to talk to him, she wants to listen to him, she wants to be needed by him. The factors involved are:

> She is obsessed with someone whom she doesn't know at all but whom she encounters from time to time.
> After meeting Scooper in Rizzoli's and finding he is a fellow bibliophile, she now thinks of them as two souls finally connecting, or as a match made in heaven.

The actress has already built up a history about Scooper because of her improvisations about him in Dr. James's office, her talks to the doctor concerning Scooper, and her meeting him in the bookstore. It was a history not from her own life, but from her imagination, and because she improvised it every week, it was as useful as her having lived it.

Improv

A dream, a fantasy, a nightmare, or any kind of expression of the character's desire, longing, wishing for a relationship with Scooper. The actress can use an imaginary figure or the actor playing Scooper. The point is to explore what it is she wants from him, with him, by him. What would she do if she had her wish and had him all to herself? Certainly when the scene in the text begins she does have him in her apartment, but life often presents us with situations that seem almost to fulfill our desires and yet elude us at the same moment. In the scene she has him, loses him, gets him back, and loses him again. But in her fantasies she never loses him because in her fantasies she is the most interesting person he has ever known. She wants to be the book he cannot put down.

The next step is to move from the improv into the scene proper. When the actress finishes her fantasy exercise she can begin the actual scene and find that she is playing actions such as:

> Being there for Scooper by listening
> Commiserating with what he's undergone and really understanding him in a way no one else would

Showing feeling for his mother
Letting him know she's the female version of Dr. James—
    a great ear you can talk to
Subtext of coming off sexy, chic, and very, very special—the
    girl you have to have

Exercise 8: Scooper's Connection to His Mother

Improv
One time an actor did a very interesting preparation for starting
the scene. He moved a piano downstage, sat at it, and played songs
for about fifteen minutes. He played very well. He sang, too. He
did all kinds of songs, from show tunes to rock and roll. When he
was finished, he and the actress, who had just done her fantasy
exercise, went right into the opening scene of the play.

Moving into the scene, both actors were very focused: she on
him, he on the images he was describing. You could almost feel the
mother, the cancer, the hospital, the apartment they were in. They
managed to get the final part of the scene to work—a good twenty
minutes of the text.

When the scene was over and I asked the actor about his preparation, he said that his mother had taught him to play the piano
and that the songs he sang were some of her favorites. That was
enough to get him connected to her, to imagine what he might
feel losing her, and when the scene started and he was describing
the cancer, he felt that his action was to talk about it to Deirdre so
it would all be better and go away.

Spec Points

Improvise what you don't know:

    Time
    Place
    Atmosphere
    Scenes or moments you had offstage

Elements of the story you are unfamiliar with
Your needs for the other character
Your character's fantasy life

Improvise on emotional areas that you do know but that have not been accessible to you for a while:

Connections you might have to the character
Analogous experiences
Your own fantasy of the character
Anything that you feel will help free you

■ ‖ ■ ‖ ■ ‖ ■ ‖ ■ ‖ ■ ‖ ■ ‖ ■ ‖ ■ ‖ ■ ‖ ■ ‖ ■ ‖ ■ ‖ ■

FREQUENTLY ASKED QUESTIONS

Q: How long should the improv be?
A: That's between you and your partner. If you are doing it for yourselves, don't put a time limit on it. If you are doing it for a director or a teacher and plan to use the improv to help you move into the written scene, you should limit yourself to ten minutes.

Q: If you are doing a play that requires no sense of weather, for example, should you bother improvising that? I mean, do you improvise everything that comes into your mind or select the essentials?
A: Don't be lazy; explore everything. You never know what you will end up using or what will have the most reverberations for you.

Q: My director hates all this stuff. If I talk about exploring something that is not in the script she gets very annoyed. What do I do?
A: Your director is using her experiences, her imagination, her mind to inform her. She does not include you

continued on page 96

continued from page 95

in her creative process. Your creative process need not
be any of her business.

Q: You mean I can do all this exploring of how I relate
to the character, creating improvs to solve certain
problems, and building an experience similar to the
character's all by myself?

A: Yes. Hopefully your scene partner is a willing
accomplice to this crime of actor's independence.

Q: What if we get lost?

A: How lost can you get? You always have the text. The
imagery of Scooper's mother's cancer is there for
him to see and to reexperience and relive.

Q: In other words, the text is always my anchor, and the
improvs are there to heighten my imagination, help me
relate to the character, and bring it all home together?

A: Correct.

Q: In the chapter on reading the text subjectively, there
was an outline on actions. It was very clear how we can
begin to choose which ones to play and to try them
out in rehearsals. It appears that in these improvs
actions can spring to life almost by themselves after
we find what we are pursuing.

A: That's right.

Q: Are we always going for actions and objectives in
improvs?

A: No. But if the improv is dealing with what you are
after from the other person, you will find yourself
playing them.

Q: So what do we do? Map out our actions and objectives
or let them just happen?

A: In a play they are given. The actor has to dig them out and try to play them. In an improv, they will happen by themselves. If you are really asking "Should we not bother consciously choosing actions when we're in a play because it's better that they just happen?" my answer would be "The art of acting is making actions appear as if you haven't predetermined them and they appear to be 'just happening.'"

Q: You mentioned the term *subtext*. How do you define it?

A: Subtext is literally what is going on underneath the words:

It could be what you really want but are not expressing.

It could be a secret that you have to keep, but it informs your behavior.

It could be a hidden agenda that is kept from the other characters or from the audience until the end.

It could be a feeling between people that is understood and needs not to be said.

It could be what a situation is all about, but it might never be directly stated.

It could be expressing that you feel one way when you actually feel the opposite.

It could be what a play really means without overtly stating that meaning.

CHAPTER 8

THE IMAGINATIVE PROCESS (2)

The improvisations in the preceding chapter show you how to prepare for the play you are working on. You will be able to use what you have found in the improv for the scene. There are times when the improv serves to be only informational: You can't directly use what you have found for the scene, but you know a lot more about the character or the situation because of the improv. But in the main, these preparations for the scene will give you an experience that you may not have had in your own life, but you have experienced in the exercise and can effectively use when acting the text.

A FEW GENERAL POINTS

As you develop your improv skills, beware of a few general points:

Listening: The true spirit of improvisation is acting through listening, and listening is a key to acting. We have to play as though we do not know what is coming next, as though we are hearing things for the first time, and as though when we do listen we respond.

Avoid Playwriting: You are not obliged to natter on and create more plot, story, or detail than is necessary. You don't have to be "interesting." If you feel you need time to think or time to respond or if you don't know what to say, take the time and be brave enough to say nothing. It's not necessary to have an answer for everything. As long as you are truly responding, silence is possible. On the other hand, don't sit there passively as your partner does all the work.

The improvs for sharing the character's experience are useful. The improvs for giving you, the actor, an analogous experience are vital. And the improvs that put your imagination inside the character's world are essential.

Finally, the actor wants to start playing the scene "for real." That means digging into actions and objectives. We've done some work on "I want." Let's develop the process of playing it further.

"I WANT" EXERCISES

"I Want" exercises help you find an emotion because they generate a strong objective.

Example

An actress is playing a role in which she is passionately jealous of her lover, who has abandoned her for another woman. Now he has returned. She wants him back, but her obstacle is her own ferocious jealousy and mistrust of him: She loves him but cannot forgive him. The actress said she is not a jealous person and had great trouble finding the right buttons within herself to press.

Exercise

She invented the following improv as a preparation for the scene. She had the actor who plays her lover play a dog, surrounded by five women who played female dogs in heat. She put herself in a position of watching the action. The females romped, chased, attacked, fought among themselves, and each tried to dominate the male dog, who enjoyed the attention and wanted to mate with all of them. The actress entered the scene as a dog and attacked all the female dogs.

Discovery

The actress said that what disturbed her most and what she now could use was her utter sense of humiliation, which was much stronger than jealousy for her. Jealousy made her feel small, demeaned, angry at herself, and confused by him. Humiliation gave her a very strong objective for playing the scene: "I want to make him pay for what he does to me."

TAPPING EMOTIONS THAT ARE ALREADY THERE

Exercise

Present something analogous from your own biography. Pull up a chair, sit down, tell a story to the group—an incident, anything that has happened to you that reminds you of something that is going on with your role in the play. An actor was working on Lenny in Pinter's *The Homecoming*. Lenny has a speech in which he talks about treating a woman violently. To help himself get to the bottom of the speech, the actor told the following "true" story. He was driving along, and a woman in her Mercedes kept cutting him off. He honked, she gave him the finger. At a long stoplight, he got out of his car. He shouted at her. She rolled down her window and started cursing him. He then socked her in the head; her glasses flew off her face, and as she cursed him some more, he got back into his car, backed up so that she wouldn't see his license, and sped off.

Did this story help him with Lenny's story? Yes. Was his story true? He said it was, but you never know.

Actors can sometimes tell stories in which the truth has been bent for the sake of overall effect.

Does it matter if this actor's story was true or not? Lenny is desperately needy for attention and loves to shock women. He displays his toughness toward them because he thinks it turns them on. So the story the actor came up with was perfect.

Discovery

Telling his "true" story made the actor realize how disturbing it was to the audience. But he enjoyed that. When he did the monologue in the scene, he played it with a very strong action of provoking his listener, but his objective was to turn her on with his cruelty. He succeeded.

THE INNER MONOLOGUE

We have thoughts going through our minds all the time. When we are interacting with another person what we are thinking is connected to what we are hearing and what we are after. Your character does not think only when he or she has a line. The inner monologue helps you capture the character's continual thinking process.

Exercise

You and your partner play the scene as written, adding what you are thinking aloud. This becomes difficult because you will have to stray from the text, but don't mind that. You can always wend your way back. The important thing is to verbalize your response to the other character (or characters). Just keep getting out your reaction to the other person. Everything that is said to you is a stimulus for a reaction. Verbalize your reaction. Speak whatever is in your head, then find the impulse to say either the line from the text or anything else you want to say. When doing this exercise it is very important that you do not mutter, mumble, or whisper.

Speak Loudly and Continually

There is no correlation between truth and inaudibility. You will express your feelings if you get them out of the back of your throat. As soon as you start expressing them, more and more will come: Like a motor that has been switched on, feelings will be generated. If, however, you are not saying anything for long periods of time, it means there is nothing going on in your head, you are not listening, you are not responding. If this happens, it means you're spacing out and not in the present tense. Activate yourself.

Don't Forget
The audience can see what's going through your character's head when you are not speaking as much as when you are. This tip is especially important in film. When the camera is on you for your reactions, it is the unsaid inner monologue that is being photographed.

Example: A friend wants to borrow your car: "May I borrow your car for a few hours?" Your answer is, "I beg your pardon?"

Your inner monologue on hearing the question is "What a nervy thing to ask!"

Say, "What a nervy thing to ask." Then say the line, "I beg your pardon?"

The inner monologue of the person asking for the loan might be, "I hate to ask, but I'm desperate. . . . May I borrow your car for a few hours?" He sees your response and says, "He just said, 'I beg your pardon?' but he's mad I asked . . ."

You can either ignore his inner monologue of "he's mad I asked" and continue with whatever impulse you have, or you can pick up on what he's just said and say, "You're damned right I'm mad you asked."

You two will practically be overlapping each other most of the time, and things will get very chaotic, but keep concentrating on listening, which will spark impulses within you. After you capture the impulses, transform them into your need to express yourself.

A Sit-Down "I Want" Exercise

The scene partners sit on chairs about six feet apart and face each other. Instead of saying any of the dialogue, each says, line for line, what he or she wants.

Example
The first four lines of *Bosoms and Neglect*:

Scooper: "Imagine a peach that had an enormous bite" can become "I want you to see it."

Deirdre: "Oh, Christ" can become "I want to pity him."
Scooper: "I'm not finished. Then. Then" can become "I want her
to know more."
Deirdre: "Calm" can become "I want him to stay steady."

You can now play the entire scene this way, substituting "I want . . ."
as impulses you are feeling moment to moment.

One Rule

Always say, "I want." Don't say, "I don't want." Put your objectives
in the most affirmative light. "I don't want to talk to him" becomes
"I refuse to talk to him." "I don't want to tell her the truth"
becomes "I want to avoid telling the truth," and so on. The reasons
for this are:

1. Playing a negative deactivates you. It disengages
   your character. Or, a continual "I don't want" makes
   your character so stubborn that no negotiation
   with you is possible. In most plays, the characters
   are bargaining, renegotiating, going through a large
   repertoire of "I wants." "I don't want" becomes
   a tedious one note.
2. Playing a negative is self-defeating for the character.
   It terminates the conflict.
3. After the conflict ends, there is no dramatic suspense for
   the members of the audience: You've lost; they're going
   to watch the winner.

PREPARATIONS TO GET TO AN ESPECIALLY DIFFICULT "I WANT"

The Dutchman by LeRoi Jones (Amiri Baraka) is a very complex
one-act play, practically replicating Greek tragedy in its unity of
time, place, and action. It is a play about race. It takes place
during a subway ride and becomes a metaphor for a young black
man's journey through hell. As Clay's train stops, he is attracted

to a sexy white girl (Lula) standing on the platform. Suddenly she's in the same car with him. She sits next to him. They talk, they flirt, tension builds between them. She is highly charged and very aggressive. She seems to know a lot about him and his friends. He is shy, very bright, and not quite sure how to take her, except that she is very attractive to him. The play goes in a circle of wordplay, crazy promises, taunts, and provocations. Lula becomes wild, spewing racial epithets one minute, luring him on with sexual promises the next. The car slowly becomes full of other passengers. She wants to dance, to rub bellies together. Clay won't dance with her, and she loses control, humiliating him in front of the other passengers. He pulls her down next to him and in his rage opens up his darkest fantasies about wanting to kill her. He can no longer tolerate her domination, her assumed control, her flagrant debasing him as a man. But he eases off, telling her that one day she will be murdered. He bends across her to retrieve his belongings. As he does so, she stabs him. She demands that the other passengers drag his dead body out of the train. They obey. She is alone. Another black young man enters. He sits a few seats in back of her. The play ends with an implication it will begin all over again.

Exercises and Improvs

1. As a team, the two actors gave a prepared fifteen-minute oral report to the group telling us about:
   a. Who the author was and what he had written
   b. The period when the play was produced and the kind of theatre it came out of
   c. The story of the play, the story of each character, and the structural elements that come from reading the text objectively (Chapter 2)
   d. Some of the author's use of language (Chapter 3) and how it gave the impression of a Greek tragedy
   e. Some beginning ideas they had for playing the material based on reading the text subjectively (Chapter 4)

2. They did preparations connected to:
   a. The subway
   b. The heat
   c. The sexual attraction between the characters
3. They improvised the entire play, going from event to event, in ten minutes. This gave them a sense of the progression of the entire piece as well as a sense of the play's intensity and the amount of energy and concentration it took to play it.

After working on the material for several weeks, the actors found that the problems in acting their roles became clear to them.

The Acting Problems for Lula

1. If the actress plays Lula like a maniac, the audience will wonder why Clay stays. She is powerfully attracted to Clay, but she is compelled to be very sharp and biting with him. She is mean and tough, but she can't scare him away, or else the play is over.
2. She has a highly neurotic agenda and is extremely dangerous. But if she hits those notes too soon, Clay will be a fool to try to deal with her. If he's such a fool, the audience loses interest in him.
3. Her objective is very buried. What does she want? She can't play that she wants to kill him. Setting herself up as a one-woman vigilante committee who wants to eradicate black men is too obvious.
4. She is very mysterious and has certain knowledge of him that she has collected, but we don't know how. Is she telling the truth? Or has she been at the same parties, knows his friends, knows his background? The author leaves these questions unanswered. The actor has to make a choice. It can remain ambiguous for the audience, but it must always be specific for the actor.

The Acting Problems for Clay

1. He is very intellectual and quite academic, but early on he is extremely naive. His progression has to be logical even though there are huge leaps of character he must take.
2. How does someone as bright as he become tantalized by Lula?
3. The racial element of wanting to be desired by a white woman, no matter how volatile she is, must become powerful for him. He is not allowed in our society to be the aggressor.

As the work developed, the moment-to-moment playing between the actors was very good. But something was missing: their objectives. Because of this, they weren't necessarily playing actions. However, every time the actress tried playing an objective, the play became predictable and obvious. When the actor tried, the result did not feel right to him or to the audience. What to do? The actors were bringing reality, sensitivity, and imagination to their work, but the play alternated between just sitting there or seeming forced and obvious.

Forgetting about the Objectives for the Time Being

As contradictory as it seems, I would say that this is one of the times when the last things you need to work on are characters' objectives. There are times when the objectives fall into place at the very end of the work. They fall into place if the work has been built on truth as far as situation is concerned and truth as far as the actors' connections to their characters are concerned. There are times when the work can be revealed to the actors only as they play it moment by moment. Imposing preconceived objectives will sometimes prevent the play from happening. (However, if you want to impose objectives right from the start and find that they work for you and the play, impose on, especially if you are lucky enough to hit on ones that are completely playable so quickly.)

■ ‖ ■ ‖ ■ ‖ ■ ‖ ■ ‖ ■ ‖ ■ ‖ ■ ‖ ■ ‖ ■ ‖ ■ ‖ ■ ‖ ■ ‖ ■ ‖ ■ ‖ ■

QUESTIONS LIKELY TO OCCUR

Q: But you've been hammering into our heads that we have to play our actions. How can we play actions that are not connected to objectives?

A: There are certain situations in which we are playing characters who don't necessarily know what they want. They exist almost on an animal level, driven by instinct or appetite, driven to survival.

Q: But you said she kills him. Why?

A: You're the actor; you find out! Why do I have to know?

Q: You don't think she kills him for a reason?

A: There is a reason why she kills him. But this is a time when you can let go and permit the play to work itself out in the playing. Sometimes it's not the worst thing in the world to learn what the play is all about late in the rehearsal. It means you have discovered it through the working process.

At other times you need a set of objectives that you completely understand before, or very soon after, you begin rehearsals.

1. Yes, you do have to know what your character wants.

2. Your character has to be motivated.

Those two elements have to be in the back of your mind all the time as mysteries to be solved. But sometimes they can't be solved immediately. And when they are solved, they can be the character's secret. You don't have to get in the audience's faces with them.

Q: What do you mean by that?

A: There is a traditional kind of drama built from cause and effect. Motivation or circumstances or environment produces the character's behavior.

continued on page 108

continued from page 107

> In another kind of play there is effect, but we are
> not sure of the cause. In other words, there is
> action or behavior, but we are not sure why. "Why"
> isn't important to the author. The problem then is
> that the actor has to fill in the "why," has to fill in
> the cause. In those instances, it takes time, because
> you are at liberty to figure out the best motivations
> through trial and error. It also takes a certain
> amount of courage to play something when the
> motivation is mysterious and almost unfathomable.
> The actor doesn't have to scream to the audience,
> "See, this is why I'm doing what I'm doing." Your
> knowing why is enough. As soon as you tell the
> audience why, the mystery is gone and so is the
> audience's interest.

The actors working on the play became more determined, and each brought in the following exercises.

Exploring Secrets

The actor playing Clay did a preparation with bawdy French poetry, using Lula as a fantasy. The actress did a fantasy of finding Clay at a party and displaying her affection for him publicly. These exercises went from the erotic to the racial to a combination of both, making it very exciting for each character.

They used the preparations of enacting their fantasies about each other to begin the scene. Things got better. The actor was driven by his desire for her, and she enjoyed stimulating his lust. Because his desire was genuine, he was able to "cool" it down, not show it so much to her, but it was there nonetheless. It was his "cooling" it that made Lula really enjoy him. But after a few pages the scene fell apart. The actress went back into ghoul mode and was so tyrannical that you had no idea why Clay didn't leave the subway car.

Consciously Working to Find Variations and Change of Tactics

When a character like Lula ends up stabbing the man she has been seducing, the actress has to find a progression and not get fixed on one or two notes. She changed action, found new impulses, switched tactics on every line. This was done in a very deliberate way—unmotivated psychologically just for the sake of itself. It is very much like what Laurence Olivier used to call "working from the outside in," which is a technique in which you apply an external first, then let it work on you internally, rather than searching for the internal to inform an external result. In this case, rather than exploring her objective, finding the actions and motivations, the actress simply imposed a scale of emotional changes on every line. The effect was to help her out of the trap of playing someone who was going to devour her victim any second. She jumped into Lula's flip-flops between being nice and being cruel, being attractive and repulsive, grooving on black men and being contemptuous of them. This exercise helped the actress see this role with greater playfulness. And when Lula is playful she is at her most dangerous: She becomes a cuddly, flesh-eating kitten, who likes to mess with a black man's mind.

Because she became genuinely volatile, a little kooky but not that dangerous to him, Clay was able to find her amusing, somewhat ridiculous, sexy, and something he could handle. And when the actor found that he could handle her, or thought that he could handle her, he latched on to his character's tragic flaw: He bit the apple of pride at making it with this outlandish white woman; and one bite turned into his own destruction.

He found a strong, workable objective: I want to be seduced by her.

(Although this objective changes in the course of the play, it was enough to get him hooked into the actress and very specific.)

The more the actress saw that the actor would permit himself to be seduced, the more tempting she made herself. Here is what finally worked for her as an objective: I want his mind, his body, and his life.

The Scene before the Scene Began

After all the research has been done, all the areas explored (if such a thing is possible), to start the scene the actor is looking for a preparation that answers:

1. Where am I coming from?
2. Where am I going?
3. Why now?

What happened before the scene began? Improvise those ten prior minutes. Invent a scenario.

Example 1: Literal
Two actors doing *The Dutchman* invent the ten minutes before they meet each other.

Example 2: Nonliteral
Each actor does a fantasy of what it would be like to be with the other person. They begin the scene.

Example 3: A Combination of Literal and Nonliteral
Each character tells the audience what he or she wants from the other characters. (The other characters do not overhear any of this.)

The Offstage Preparation

Doing the preceding exercises will help you go right into the scene, your wants and actions generating themselves. The improvs help you experience the emotional life of the character and your relationship with the other characters. All of these elements will put you in the right place to begin the scene: You know where you're coming from; you know where you're going; and you definitely know why you are on the stage now!

After you've found the one or two preparations that really help you get the scene to work more effectively, you will be able to use them each time you do the scene, without having to go through the exercise again. It will exist as stored music within you. Now, however, you know where the buttons are that help you play it.

As a result of all our work so far on autodrama, text, language, and imagination, the actor should be able to ask the following questions when beginning the work:

1. Have I read the play fully? More than once?
2. Am I clear on the story?
3. Do I have any idea what the play is about? What's confusing?
4. How do I relate to the play?
5. Where does my character fit in?
6. How do I relate to the character?
7. What problems do I think I will have?
8. What kind of actor's research will I be doing?
9. What kind of offstage preparations do I want to try?
10. Do I have much of an idea what the character wants?
11. Are the character's objectives and actions overt or buried inside the text? Are they a combination of both?
12. Besides doing a good job, what are my immediate goals with this role?

    a. Developing a deeper use of my own biography to relate to the character
    b. Solving the problems I had the last time out
    c. Improving my inner monologue skills
    d. Working more on the "I want" exercises
    e. Being more spontaneous and more courageous in my improvs
    f. Finding preparations that get me going in the scene
    g. Continuing to work on actions: I've almost got it now.

PART 3

THE CHARACTERIZATION

Synthesizing tools and process into the specifics of character:

■ Ways of exploring character

■ Imagining an interview with your character

■ Solving acting problems with your character in rehearsal: a diary

■ Asking questions about yourself and your character: a dialogue

CHARACTERIZATION (1)

All roads lead here: text, language, story, and the actor's imagination connect and help you portray the role. There's a lot of ourselves we will use—a lot of our feelings, experiences, and imaginings. But finally the aim is to become some other person called "the character." We use ourselves to become someone else. That is, we pretend to become someone else. We mustn't mistake acting for having psychotic episodes. A certain amount of fallout from the character currently being played is bound to affect the actor in daily life, and raking up certain feelings can be grueling, which might be why actors do not want to play certain roles, or, if they do play them, they prefer a limited run. But most good actors are very keen observers of other people as well as of themselves and usually know reality from fantasy.

TECHNIQUES

Read the play for clues. If you regard your character as a mystery to be solved, then every element of the play becomes a clue to the solution.

1. A subjective and objective reading is necessary.
2. How does the author describe your character?
3. Do the other characters in the play have varying opinions about your character? What are they?
4. After much process work such as improvisation, make sure you have learned the lines correctly, remembering that the details are in the language the author has given you.

RESEARCHING

You can't know too much. An actress friend was furious because of the clothes "they" had put her character in. Her husband said, "What difference does it make? You're a voiceover for a cartoon." She said, "It makes all the difference in the world. *My character would never wear that!*" She was most likely right.

Physical Circumstances

Physical reality often creates behavior. Explore where the character lives, what clothes are worn, what it's like during different times of the year, what conversations were likely to be spoken. Go to the library, to museums, to art galleries; study films; investigate what it was like to live in your character's world. Touch, taste, smell, sight, and hearing have to be fine-tuned and brought to bear as they affect character.

Class

This is often a neglected component of the actor's conceptualizing the role. Social stratification and where your character fits in are elements to be reckoned with. The conflicts within *A Streetcar Named Desire* are built on class and on the characters' conception of class. Stanley is working class and proud of it. Blanche, the teacher whose background is landed gentry, has great pretensions to aristocratic pedigree. Stella is in the middle, straddling both classes and pulled in both directions: her loyalty to her husband versus her loyalty to her sister.

One of the reasons why the British do Chekhov so adeptly is because they have an inherent understanding of class strata. What is a peasant? What is an aristocrat? What is a bourgeois merchant? Within each class there are many specifics, and it is important that the actor doesn't head for clichés. Not all bourgeois merchants are boors, fat, and lascivious. Not all aristocrats prance around and speak affectedly. The trick is for the actor not only to capture the class of the character but also to find something original within it. You can play Kowalski as a crotch-scratching philistine because that is what you think the working class is all about. But you will miss the wit, humor, and surprising sensitivity that Tennessee Williams has endowed him with—traits that are complete surprises once the audience gets to know him.

Shakespeare, of course, is brimming with class differences, but how many times have you seen an actor play a rustic in a Shakespeare comedy and intone his lines as though he were the duke of York? If your particular rustic thinks he's the duke of York and puts on those airs, it might be funny. If not, you are acting very generalized Shakespeare and have no sense of who you are supposed to be. You'll just delude yourself into thinking that "This is how they talk Shakespeare."

Interviews

If you are doing a period play, you will have to rely on newspapers, diaries, and archival sources for certain kinds of information. However, if you are playing a contemporary person, interview people who have had a shared experience with your character. Police officers, lawyers, and doctors are usually very forthcoming. If you are playing a gangster, it may not be easy or safe to find a person to interview, but chances are you can pull together enough material to understand such a person and find out how he or she ticks. If you're playing Mary Tyrone in *Long Day's Journey into Night*, it is not necessary that your research include trying morphine any more than it would be necessary for you, when playing Medea, to murder your own children to see what she went through. But people with chemical addictions, after they are in treatment, are sometimes willing to talk about what it's like.

Find out why people went into their particular profession, what gives them pleasure, what's frustrating, and so on. Talk to them about your specific character. They'll have interesting things to tell you. And in talking to these people you might be able to identify with your character in a new way.

Exploring Ego

What is your character's sense of self-worth? Big ego, small ego, no ego? Many characters in Chekhov undergo a crisis of ego. Their image of themselves varies between self-love and self-hatred. Trepleff in *The Sea Gull* (which will be examined more specifically in the next chapter) begins by believing he has reinvented the theatre and is quite proud of himself, but his play fails. He kills a sea gull and, not deriving any satisfaction from that, tries to kill himself. He eventually gives in to his most destructive side—the side of him that negates all self-worth: suicide.

Nina, on the other hand, works out her torn ego by alternating between imagining herself being a helpless sea gull and being an actress. She finally realizes she is an actress and must go on with her life.

Hamlet is practically a meditation on one man's ego. Shakespeare loved villains such as Iago, Richard III, and Edmund in *King Lear* who take their twisted self-loathing and transform it into brilliant plotting to outwit their enemies. These are characters who absolutely fall head over heels in love with themselves because they know they're so much smarter than anyone else.

Example of a very healthy ego
The gentleman caller in *The Glass Menagerie* on first reading seems quite full of himself. He's practically a salesman, pitching self-confidence. He's found something in his life and wants to share it with Laura.

> **Jim:** . . . You know what my strong advice to you is? Think of yourself as superior in some way! (*Unconsciously glances at himself in the mirror*) Everybody excels in some thing. Some in many! All you've got to do is discover in what! Take me for instance. (*He adjusts his tie in the mirror.*) My interest happens to lie in electrodynamics. I'm taking a course in radio engineering at night school, Laura, on top of a fairly responsible job at the warehouse. I'm taking that course and studying public speaking.
> **Laura:** Ohhhh.

Jim: Because I believe in the future of television! I wish to be ready to go up right along with it. Therefore, I'm planning to get in on the ground floor. In fact I've already made the right connections and all that remains is for the industry itself to get under way! Full steam . . .

(His eyes are starry)

Knowledge—ZSSSSSP! Money—ZSSSSSP!—Power! That's the cycle democracy is built on! (*His attitude is convincingly dynamic. LAURA stares at him, even her shyness eclipsed in her absolute wonder. He suddenly grins*) I guess you think I think a lot of myself.

Language

As discussed earlier, language has many uses. It is the most tangible aspect of character. Ntozake Shange, the author of *for colored girls who have considered suicide/when the rainbow is enuf* . . . calls that play a "choreopoem." It is a powerful piece of theatre in which seven women relate their lives and feelings to each other and to the audience. An example:

> *lady in red*
> *without any assistance or guidance from you*
> *i have loved you assiduously for 8 months 2 wks & a day*
> *i have been stood up four times*
> *i've left 7 packages on yr doorstep*
> *forty poems 2 plants & 3 handmade notecards i left*
> *town so i cd send to you have been no help to me*
> *on my job*
> *you call at 3:00 in the mornin on weekdays*
> *so i cd drive 27 1/2 miles cross the bay before i go to work*
> *charmin charmin*
> *but yu are of no assistance*
> *i want you to know*
> *this waz an experiment*
> *to see how selfish i cd be*

if i wd really carry on to snare a possible lover
if i waz capable of debasin my self for the love of another if i cd
stand not being wanted
when i wanted to be wanted
& i cannot
so
with no further assistance & no guidance from you
i am endin this affair
this note is attached to a plant
i've been waterin since the day i met you
you may water it
yr damn self

The actress playing the lady in red can mine, through the language of the poem, a wealth of detail about this character. We can see the character as someone who is funny, proud, and very hurt. When she says the whole thing was "an experiment/to see how selfish i cd be" she reveals herself as a person who wants her dignity back, who is reversing roles in order not to be subservient to this man again. The selection can certainly be interpreted in different ways, but the choice of words, a particular kind of vernacular, the built-in rhythms give the actress a strong sense of her character.

Motivation

There are actors who cannot cross from stage right to stage left unless they know what motivates them to do so. If the script calls for the actress to cry, she may be unable to if she doesn't know why. Without reasons, actors are hesitant because they do not want to be arbitrary. There are characters whose motivation is very clearly laid out by the author—authors such as Ibsen, Shaw, Shakespeare, and the Greeks, among others. This is the cause-and-effect scenario that was discussed in the preceding chapter.

However, in the plays of Samuel Beckett and Harold Pinter, for example, motivation is ambiguous. Why two hobos are sitting in an open field waiting for Godot is not explicit. In that case the actors have to invent specific reasons. They cannot be general. If they haven't found motivation for themselves, they will not feel the need to generate the play's action. What they have chosen as their motivation may not ever be known by the audience.

As we discussed in the example of *The Dutchman,* the actor has explored the character's behavior, that is, what the character is doing to get what he wants and why he's doing it. But the audience does not always have to know the "*why?*" The author intends the audience to do some work as well.

Exercise: "How I Spent My (Fill in the Blank) Vacation"

After spring break, Christmas, or summer, consider a ten-minute presentation in which you play yourself and four other people you dealt with during this period. Observe the following:

> What is it that those who are close to you want?
> What are they doing to get what they want?
> What motivates them?
> How do you behave with these people?

The exercise not only will help you play the actions and objectives of people you know, but it will give you the opportunity to explore their motivation. Also, you have to transform yourself into four characters as well as play yourself.

More Exercises

Observation and Real-Life Studies

The world around us is the actor's best sketch pad:

1. Observe people you know or those who catch your interest for the first time. Try to capture their characteristics: their movements, rhythm, the way they talk or bear themselves in silence. People become garments you can wear. Every bus ride has at least one person you can study.

    When you're doing a real-life study be careful that you aren't observed. You'll make both of you very uncomfortable.

Bring your portrayals to class. See how much you've captured. The tendency is to do someone you've found sitting, eating, or just being still. After a few of these, go for people who are active. Observe how their bodies work. Look for strengths, such as hands, arms, or legs. Try to determine where the center of focus of that person lies. Sometimes the focus is elusive: You might think that a workman's center of focus is all in his hands, but it may very well be in his eyes. Don't make too many assumptions about anyone, otherwise you'll get trapped into clichés. People are far more interesting than they are stereotyped to be.

2. Sometimes a person may remind you of an animal. You might want to go to the zoo to refer to that animal. Playing the animal can be very useful. A certain kind of monkey, for example, may help you find a dynamic that is just right for the person you are trying to capture. Animals help free us. Capture rhythms, volatility, power in both attack and repose.

   However, if you are using an animal for either a real-life study or for an aid in a part you are playing, you will usually get tripped up after you start using the dialogue of the text. The way the animal behaves and the way people speak are often difficult to fuse. Don't use the text literally. Improvise a special language or make sounds you think your animal would make in the situation.

3. After you have come to enjoy observing people and doing what you recall of them, go a step further. Imagine what they are thinking. It's not important that the actor invent an entire, complex play to put in a character's head. Most people think in a loop: a few thoughts over and over. Keep it simple. Try to figure out what the character wants in the situation and verbalize those desires.

4. It is helpful to keep a scrapbook of anything that you feel might be of interest later: faces for makeup studies, photographs of people in situations that are personally evocative to you, postcards of paintings in various museums—anything. It's like having a songwriter's trunk: One day you'll use that song (character) in a show.

Two Hints

When you are searching for your character in rehearsal, you will never find the complete person from observation or that one animal that will make the whole part come together. You will usually find from one person a pair of hands that could be useful, from another person the walk. Your final portrait will usually end up being a composite of observed and imagined elements.

Just make sure the character you come up with belongs in the play you're working on.

Nonliteral pathways into character. Getting out of your head and putting the character into your body.

How does this character move? The physical coloring the actor brings to the role helps tell the character's story.

1. Find some music of the period and as you play it, just let yourself move as the character would. After a while your character might imagine being onstage doing a solo dance concert. Change the music, imagine your character in different situations—move, dance—nothing you're doing has to be "real" or literal.

    Secrets, inner conflicts, dreams, private yearnings can all be tapped into through music and dance and gesture. It's important to get your instincts going in this direction, because sometimes the smallest discovery can open up the whole role. There might be a tangible object, symbol or icon that is pivotal for your character. You need to unlock the relationship.

2. How does money make manner? So many characters want money, need money, lose money, can't get enough money, borrow money, steal money, are in trouble because of money. Use money as a central element in a dance or a dream. How does your character's body respond to it? Try a wish fulfillment fantasy as money goes through your hands. What's a penny like in your pocket? What's a penny like found on the floor? Do people with real money move differently than people who pretend to have money, but don't? Find a piece of music that makes you move in a way

you don't care about money. What's the happiness money can buy? Express the happiness in movement or dance.

**Distancing yourself from the role in order
to get closer to it.**
An effective way to take a good look at the character you are playing is to switch roles. It will give you a whole new perspective.

Exercise: You are playing Biff and your partner is playing Happy in the bedroom scene from *Death of a Salesman*. Exchange roles. It's not necessary to know Happy's lines exactly, because you can improvise. As you are playing Happy, you will be very fine-tuned to what Biff is doing and how effectively he impresses you. In short, you will be able to take an objective look at the guy and begin to see who he is from another perspective. When you return to playing Biff, chances are you will then see things from Happy's perspective and realize what you have to do and how you have to do it to get what you're after from him.

**Gaining perspective on your role can also be achieved
by playing both roles.**

Exercise: Use hand puppets, or socks. Biff is the right hand, Happy is the left hand. Play the dialogue of the scene as you articulate the puppets. You might find this frees you to express your character more fluidly than when you were trying to put the character inside yourself.

The Extended Character Exercise

Putting a character onto the stage for an extended period of time gives you the opportunity to stretch your imagination.

Exercise
Choose from a play or a novel or from history a character you'd like to work on. Or invent a character of your own. Start with a five-minute sketch of the person. Get some feedback, digest it

over a period of time, and when you are ready, see if you can't do a ten-minute presentation. When an actor is in a play, he or she lives with the character for months at a time: the preparation, the rehearsal, the run of the production. The extended character exercise gives you this opportunity with two advantages:

> You have no constraint of time.
> The character and his or her presentation are of your own invention.

If you are having trouble with language, create a character who is very verbal. If you need to work on releasing body tension, create a character through the language of movement and don't use words. If you are a loudmouth or are very shy, find an opposite to play. If you know what some of your problems are as an actor, create a character who will help you move out of those problems, or confront those problems head on. You can also develop a character who is of the opposite sex and of a different race. Men playing women has a long tradition in the theatre. Women playing men has its own history, especially in opera. Color-blind casting is still somewhat delicate, but no one should rule out what we can act.

Example: A student decided to portray the artist Andy Warhol. He never met Warhol, never saw him in person. There was something about Warhol that the student found fascinating. He began by reading Warhol's diaries and started inventing improvisations. He wore a white wig, tight pants that accentuated his thinness, and boots that gave him a careful, delicate walk. The world that the student created was The Factory—Warhol's studio where he painted, interviewed people, made some of his films. The student used the other actors in the class as Warhol's friends and coworkers.

It was very funny. But the actor wasn't quite sure where he was going with it. He dug in and did more research. He saw many of the films Warhol made, studied the art, read the criticism, went through the history of the 1960s and 1970s. He improvised scenes in which he interviewed other characters with Warhol's theory that everyone is interesting for fifteen minutes. He could find very little of Warhol on tape or film, so he had to make up what wasn't documented. Still he was unsettled. He just didn't know what he was really looking for. He thought of dropping the whole idea and finding someone else to work on.

One day he used the whole class to improvise an afternoon at The Factory. He based the scene on information he had read in Warhol's *Successful Guide to Partying.* He had three men in bed, various women making themselves up and trying on costumes, some people being interviewed, and an artist was painting as "Andy" moved among them, watching, taking it all in.

When he finished he was asked if he had found "that certain something" he was looking for. He said he had. He had found Warhol's complete voyeurism exciting. We usually think of voyeurism as something very passive, something unactable. But the student found an inner energy, a compulsive need to devour everything his character observed. The act of being the observer was what he felt Warhol lived for.

The student developed the character study into a fifteen-minute piece at the end of the year. A friend of Warhol attended. When it was over, the student asked, "Was that anything like Andy Warhol at all?" The friend of Warhol said, "Exactly! I thought you said you didn't know him."

■ || ■ || ■ || ■ || ■ || ■ || ■ || ■ || ■ || ■ || ■ || ■ || ■ || ■ || ■ || ■

FREQUENTLY ASKED QUESTIONS

Q: I always think everyone in rehearsal is much cleverer than I am at characterization. They seem to come up with walks, mannerisms, accents, funny bits of business much quicker. What can I do?

A: Some actors are that way. They latch on to externals very fast, and it helps them. The trap, of course, is that these externals can lead you astray: You'll be stuck with a walk that is wrong for the character, an accent that is not accurate, and funny business that gets no laughs.

continued on page 126

continued from page 125

Other actors find their characters as a slow metamorphosis into them. By dress rehearsal something happens: Their reading, their researching, their sense of the language, their costumes, the feel of the lights, and the excitement of the audience about to come transform them into the character.

It's best to allow some gestation period for your character to evolve and not to impose demands for immediate results.

Q: What if I'm just doing scene work as opposed to the whole play—how much of the character do I have to find?

A: It depends on what the assignment is. Listen carefully to the teacher or the director. Some teachers do not like instant results imposed on the character. Another teacher might want you to do "quick sketches" of a character to help you externalize, that is, to help you get feelings you have inside you pushed out and demonstrated.

Q: Why are some actors always the same in every role they play?

A: They don't think they are the same. They believe that every second has been filled specifically as that character. It's not necessary to go into complete disguise for every role. How far to go is determined by you, the director, and the designers.

Q: I enjoy characterizing when I can be very physical. I still have problems with long speeches. I drop out of character and become the actor who is self-consciously aware of being boring.

A: Get a group of friends together and start a "reader's theatre." Read poetry to each other and to a small audience. Find some short stories that interest you. Read them aloud. A short story will give you the

chance to speak in different voices: the narration
and all the characters. Eventually you will realize that
you are holding the stage in the very way that had
frightened you the most.

Q: What about characters who have long monologues—
any advice?

A: Three things:

1. Whom are you talking to: the audience, another
   character, or yourself?
2. What do you want by giving this speech?

   If you are talking to the members of the audience, you have something specific in mind: getting them on your side, confessing secrets, enter-
   taining them, and so on.

   If you are talking to another character, you
   want something from that character. Your speech
   is built as a series of tactics or actions. Find those.
   Long speeches are built like scenes: They are full
   of changing actions and topics.

   If you are talking to yourself, you are trying to
   overcome an obstacle or solve a problem.
3. As we have seen, speeches are conditioned by an
   external event, but equally important is the fact that
   speeches invariably contain a recognition or an internal event: That is, something happens to the character onstage as a result of the speech. The lady in red
   in *for colored girls* can have made up her mind to
   break it off with her man. She has the argument all
   figured out. It's in her head. After she goes into the
   speech she recognizes that she finally means what
   she is saying and will finally do what she has been
   threatening—end the relationship:

   > *i've been waterin since the day i met you*
   > *you may water it*
   > *yr damn self.*

(HARACTERIZATION (2)

THE ACTOR INTERVIEWS HIS CHARACTER (AN EXERCISE)

A young actor is cast as Trepleff in Chekhov's *The Sea Gull*. Act I has been blocked, and the company is about to tackle Act II. In this act, Trepleff enters carrying a sea gull that he's shot offstage. In the third act, he attempts to shoot himself offstage. The actor knows that:

1. He has to find the most playable actions.
2. He has to find actions that are connected to a strong objective.
3. And with all that, he needs logical motivation so the audience will have some understanding of his character.

He's not too sure about the choices he's made in Act I. Because of that, he feels a little lost about how to begin Act II. So many choices! And which are the right ones? He wishes that Trepleff were in the room with him so he could ask some very direct questions. Because the actor is always questioning his character, why not use your imagination to see what would happen if you hypothetically had your character in the same room with you and you could ask anything you wanted? Really take a good look at "who" you are playing. In other words, externalize your intuition and your curiosity by having a dialogue: you and Trepleff.

The Situation

Trepleff is a young man who lives off his actress mother on her country estate. He has prepared a staging of his new play, which is symbolic, metaphorical, and the antithesis of the kind of theatre his mother performs. His leading lady is a young woman, Nina, who lives across the lake. He seems to adore her. His play begins— an outdoor production for his relatives, his mother, and her latest lover—but his sulphuric smoke effects get out of control. His mother makes fun of the whole event; Trepleff stops the play and runs off in anger.

In Act II he enters, carrying a sea gull he has just shot. He sees Nina, who is sitting on a bench. They haven't seen each other since the failure of his play.

(Trepleff enters, without a hat, carrying a gun and a dead sea gull.)

Trepleff: Are you here alone?
    Nina: Alone. (*Trepleff lays the sea gull at her feet*) What does that mean?
Trepleff: I was low enough to kill this sea gull. I lay it at your feet.
    Nina: What's the matter with you? (*Picks up sea gull and looks at it*)
Trepleff: It's the way I'll soon end my own life.
    Nina: I don't even recognize you.
Trepleff: Yes, ever since I stopped recognizing you. You've changed toward me. Your eyes are cold. You hate to have me near you.
    Nina: You are so irritable lately, and you talk . . . it's as if you were talking in symbols. And this sea gull, I suppose that's a symbol, too. Forgive me, but I don't understand it. (*Lays the sea gull on the seat*) I'm too simple to understand you.
Trepleff: This began that evening when my play failed so stupidly. Women will never forgive failure. I've burnt it all, every scrap of it. If you only knew what I'm going through! Your growing cold to me is terrible, unbelievable; it's as if I had suddenly waked and you found this lake dried up and sunk in the ground. You say you are too simple to understand me. Oh, what is there to understand? My play didn't catch your fancy, you despise my kind of imagination, you already consider me commonplace, insignificant, like so many others. (*Stamping his foot*) How well I understand it all, how

I understand it. It's like a spike in my brain, may it be damned along with my pride, which is sucking my blood, sucking it like a snake. (*He sees Trigorin, who enters reading a book*) Here comes the real genius, he walks like Hamlet, and with a book, too. (*Mimicking*) "Words, words, words." This sun has hardly reached you, and you are already smiling, your glance is melting in his rays. I won't stand in your way. (*He goes out*)

The actor is not sure how to play this scene. He imagines he is interviewing his character.

The Interview

Actor: Do you like what I did in the run-through of the first act of *The Sea Gull* today?

Character: May I be frank?

Actor: Please.

Character: I'm a passionate man, and you play me like set decoration, a passive bore. I am not passive.

Actor: How passionate is anyone in Chekhov? I was searching for the mood, the autumnal qualities . . .

Character: You make me unbearably tedious. No one plays Trepleff right. I'm part of a dramatic story. Yes, Chekhov was dramatic! He didn't write mood pieces. He wrote plays! I'm a vivid character with passionate desires, and you make me a boring, whining fool.

Actor: I see you as a kind, gentle man.

Character: You're turning me into everything my mother thinks I am: a useless nerd. I am not a nerd. I am a fighter, struggling for life.

Actor: You are?

Character: Everyone misreads me! Where's the conflict? Dramatic stories are built on conflict. Give me conflict, not mood. Give me drama, not atmosphere! You've turned me into a bowl of cold mashed potatoes. [pause] You haven't quite figured me out yet, have you?

Actor: To be honest, I haven't. I have glimmers, but nothing concrete.

Character: Don't you know what I want? Don't you know what I'm after?

Actor: You want to be a writer, right?

Character: Weak, weak. Well, no wonder you have me doing nothing most of the time. When you find out what I'm after, then you'll see all the things I'm doing to get it.

Actor: I was hoping I'd get a clearer picture of you in Act II.

Character: I love my entrance, coming in with the dead bird in one hand and the shotgun in the other. What are you going to do about that entrance?

Actor: Do?

Character: Do. Before you go on.

Actor: Well, let's see. I go to the prop table, pick up the shotgun and the sea gull. I try to relax. Get my breathing in order. Wait for my cue and enter!

Character: That's what you do. You, the actor! What do I do, the character. There's no prop table in the woods. What was I doing before I saw Nina? Use your imagination!

Actor: You shot a sea gull. It's in your hand.

Character: Why did I shoot a sea gull?

Actor: I'm sure you'd really have preferred to shoot your mother. Or shoot her boyfriend, Trigorin, who was fascinated with Nina. Instead you shot a sea gull. You were angry.

Character: Yes, I was that angry, I shot a damned sea gull, and how do you think that makes me feel to have the poor dead thing in my hand?

Actor: Awful.

Character: Wretched, stupid, ashamed.

Actor: Everything makes you feel ashamed.

Character: Not everything. I'm ten times a better writer than my mother's boyfriend.

Actor: You are such an odd mixture of ego and no ego. You think you've reinvented the theatre one minute and feel totally worthless the next. When you are not feeling shame you are feeling arrogant. What is all that about? I can't resolve that.

Character: You want everything in a neat box? Enjoy my duality.
Characters like myself are paradoxes. Most interesting
people are.

Actor: Why didn't you bury the sea gull or leave it behind?
Why are you walking around holding it?

Character: Let's reconstruct this. Motivation: Out of rage for
my mother's behavior and humiliation over my play,
I shoot a sea gull. I pick it up, not knowing what to
do with the poor thing. Where am I going?

Actor: You are going onstage.

Character: *You* are going onstage. I'm in the woods. I see Nina
sitting on a bench. I haven't seen her since the aborted
performance.
Objective: I want to talk to her, I want to tell her I
don't understand what is happening to me, I want to
tell her I need her.
Obstacle: I don't know what she thinks of me.
Has any of this ever happened to you in your life?
Can you imagine what it would be like to face a girl
you are fond of, a girl who witnessed the audience
laugh your work off the stage?

Actor: Is that what it's like?

Character: I'm just trying to get you to use your imagination and
come up with things I'm feeling.

Actor: I would probably want to fall to my knees and cry.

Character: Yes. But I can't. I'm a grown man.

Actor: I would want her to understand me, soothe me,
comfort me.

Character: There you go. Very playable. Try those.

Actor: But maybe I suspect she feels I deserve the scorn for
my failed play. Maybe she's now on everyone else's
side. If that's the case, I would feel different about
her. I would really do what I could to hurt her.

Character: Possibly.

Actor: So which is it?

Character: Which is what?

Actor: Am I needful of her, or do I want to hurt her?

Character: Try both.

Actor: I have to play one thing at a time. I can't play both things at once, can I? Help me.

Character: I want self-esteem. I want Nina. I don't care about Nina, she's as bad as my mother. I don't care about my mother; I hate her. Of course I don't hate my mother; I love her. Why should I love my mother— she doesn't love me! Yes. No. Oh, forget it, I don't want to talk about either of those women. Why should either care about me? I don't deserve anything!

Actor: You're right. You are a very passionate man! And your mind is always going in opposite directions. Thanks for showing me your inner monologue.

Character: Let's go back to the scene. I'm trudging along with a gun in one hand and a dead sea gull in the other. I see Nina. I'm surprised.

Actor: You say, "Are you alone?"

Character: What's underneath that simple greeting?

Actor: I can see that she's alone. So I have the following choices:
1. I can play the line rhetorically, to get a conversation started.
2. I can play the line to make sure no one else is coming.
3. I can play the line like I have a lot to tell her and am making sure we won't be interrupted.
4. I can play the line as a setup to shocking her by throwing the dead creature at her feet.

Character: Choices, choices. I love this. Which do you think it is?

Actor: You're the character; you tell me.

Character: I like choices that show my impulsive side. I'm still angry since the fiasco of my play and want to hurt everyone and everything. Yet I need Nina very, very much.

Actor: She looks at you and says, "Alone."

Character: Then she looks at me and sees this dead sea gull in my hand, and I'm filled with shame at what I've done. I lay it at her feet. I want her to see what I've done, show her my dark deed, because she'll understand. We were so close before my play was laughed at. She'll understand what misunderstood artists go through.

Actor: She says, "What does that mean?"

Character: I confess to her, "I was low enough to kill this sea gull. I lay it at your feet."

Actor: She says, "What's the matter with you?" and picks it up.

Character: The minute she says that to me I see that things are hopeless, I feel she doesn't understand anything about me.

Actor: Your next line is "It's the way I'll soon end my own life."

Character: Poor me.

Actor: I'm not going to feel sorry for you. I'm not going to make you self-pitying.

Character: Good. Self-pitying actors are unwatchable. They just want to make the audience cry.

Actor: Maybe you want to scare her when you talk of suicide.

Character: Hmmm. You think?

Actor: Maybe you want to scare her into feeling something for you.

Character: Those are interesting choices.

Actor: Which should I play?

Character: Do them both.

Actor: I keep telling you that I can play only one thing at a time.

Character: Try one one day and the other the next. Explore each one; see what happens.

Actor: After you make your confession, she says, "I don't even recognize you" and . . .

Character: Imagine that you look for compassion and you get a blank wall. Something inside me happens . . .

Actor: You go from needing her desperately, needing her to understand you, to recognizing the fact that she doesn't understand you at all. Your rage returns, and all you want to do is hurt her the way she has just hurt you. And this goes back and forth between you . . .

Character: Conflict, dear boy, conflict. It's what I keep telling you. The essence of any story, especially a dramatic one, is conflict. I have been conflicted within myself: I think

I'm great, I think I'm garbage; I love my mother, I hate my mother; I love the theatre, I think it's all phony and artificial. And now conflict between two people, Nina and me.

Actor: You want something she can't give you.

Character: Love! It's what I want more than anything, but I can't get it from my mother, and I can't get it from Nina.

Actor: So the next thing that happens in this scene is—and you could say this is why the scene is in the play—is . . .

Character: Yes?

Actor: You tell me.

Character: I want to hear you say it.

Actor: I completely realize that I am unloved.

Character: You said, "I." You said, "I am unloved."

Actor: You like that?

Character: You are becoming me. Fabulous.

Actor: You've given me a great deal to think about. I'll try those choices, see how they work. When I enter the scene and see Nina I will play:

1. I am glad to see her.
2. I need her.
3. I want her.
4. I long for her understanding and her love.
5. I realize she can give me nothing.

It's a good progression.

Character: Try talking to me more often.

At this point the actor concluded the following:

1. I was playing qualities, not actions, thereby creating a very passive character. The character wants to fight.
2. There is no conflict when I haven't chosen strong actions and objectives. I have to go back to Chapter 4 to the qualifications that make an objective strong:
   a. It must be attained.
   b. Something must be at stake (in this case, Trepleff's life).

     c. It wants to be fulfilled now.

     d. I need my character to selfishly pursue it.

3. There always has to be an offstage preparation. I can't drop out of my imagination before entering.
   Remember:
   a. Where am I coming from?
   b. Where am I going?
   c. And why now?

4. I shouldn't overlook the contradictions within a character, even though I can play only one thing at a time.

5. My character demands that I use my imagination or life experience to relate to what he's going through.

6. I have to stop worrying about the "right" choice and trust that if what I choose doesn't work, I can come up with something else.

7. I am beginning to see how much actually has to happen on the stage to my character. Chekhov compresses actions, objectives, obstacles, and an event that alters the character's behavior all within a dozen lines or so. I really have to be on my toes and let nothing slip by.

8. This scene is a good example of how an objective changes and how real conflict begins because the character can't get what he wants: love, understanding, contact.

9. I said it before, but I have to keep saying it: Something is at stake. If I can keep that in my head, I will stop playing passively.

10. I'm beginning to see what subtext is: things that I can't say to Nina; the way we really affect each other; my character's confusion and anxieties . . . what I really want.

11. Imagining this interview has made me dig deeper.

PUTTING IT TOGETHER (1)

The following is a diary (fictitious) of an actress who is relatively new to the profession and has been cast as Stella in a regional theatre production of *A Streetcar Named Desire*. The diary is a helpful technique for the actress to express her private thoughts. She very much wants to do a good job and is trying to pull together all the elements of her training: self, text, language, imagination, and character. However, as she attempts to live the life of her character, she discovers an area of Stella that she is resisting: being dominated by Stanley. Fighting an aspect of your character is not unusual. The problem is usually solved in the following ways:

1. You forget about it and hope you'll be all right by opening night.
2. You fake it, finding some level of reality that can appear acceptable to the audience but that in no way touches you.
3. You work very hard to find why you are resisting a full commitment to the character and how to fully engage yourself.

The actress's training helped her realize that when the time came to solve certain acting problems, only she could do it. This chapter and the next one, Putting It Together (2), suggest methods to achieve it.

THE DIARY OF AN ACTRESS

Dear Diary,

I'm on the train up to the Rep to play Stella in *A Streetcar Named Desire*. Finally, I'll be acting in a Tennessee Williams play. If only I had some advance notice. They told me yesterday! I suppose the girl they really wanted dropped out. But I don't care. I got the job. And what a play! More like a poem, really. If only I weren't so unprepared to begin tomorrow. Hope the acting company is good.

Kay

Diary,

After doing the Equity business, the actors were whisked off for costume fittings. The director is from England. It's obvious she's disappointed with me and probably wishes her first choice had worked out. The actress who plays Blanche is very temperamental. (She's played the role before.) Our Stanley is nice enough as a person but doesn't seem to use deodorant.

The director announced she was going to show us the movie version. I slipped out. So did May (our Blanche). I don't want to see what another actress did with the part. I want to create my own version.

Kay

Diary,

We read the play twice this afternoon. Everyone is very good. I'm terrible. The director hates me. I'm going to sleep. (If I can.)

Kay

Diary,

Up at dawn, grabbed the script, read the whole play again. Overwhelmed by its beauty again. But Stella is so dull. Everyone else so colorful. I'm not going to think about it. I often feel this way in the beginning. My instincts tell me that all I need to do to find this role is listen. Stella is a great listener.

Kay

P.S. I'm very frightened of something and don't know what it is.

Diary,

Yesterday the director took me aside and said she expected me to "bring things of my own to this role." She said, "Don't expect me to spoon-feed you, dearie." Which is fine with me, at least it's better than a director who dictates every breath. May, our Blanche, keeps borrowing money from me. (She's not turning into the role offstage as well, is she?)

Kay

Diary,

Why is everyone's character much clearer than mine? I know that women like Stella still exist, but she's almost like Tennessee Williams's fantasy of what a good woman is. Her main function in life is serving Stanley sexually. She's so nice, so understanding, so damned radiant! It makes me sick. I wonder if it's possible to play a person whose behavior strikes you this way. (I'm an actress—of course I can!)

Kay

P.S. Maybe I'm just intimidated by the play, by its glorious history and legendary performances . . . Marlon Brando, Vivien Leigh . . .

Diary,

I stupidly let slip some of my private reservations about Stella to the director, who looked at me scornfully and said, "I haven't got a feminist on my hands playing this part, have I?" I said of course she didn't.

What am I to make of Stella? Stanley hits her, he calls, she runs, he makes love to her, she's in complacent bliss for days. It's almost as if she were defined by Stanley.

Kay

Diary,

1. It fascinates me that this play was produced only two years before Arthur Miller's *Death of a Salesman*. Similar sensibilities . . . post-Depression, post-WW2. The working class, the struggle to "make it" financially. Willy in *Salesman* does nothing but lie to himself (and everyone else), Blanche lies to herself (and everyone else).

In this long story about truth and revelation and madness, where does my character fit in?

2. Although the play is like a long poem, everyone's poetry is quite different. Blanche and Stanley are worlds apart in language styles, yet this friction helps put them in the same play.

The language of Stella is direct, clean. . . . Watch out for hidden booby traps: A Southern dialect that is not specific; a dialect that affects clear speech; a dialect that is more like a pig farmer than a Mississippi lady. I do sometimes fall into Blanche's rhythm, and when I do, it sounds like two Scarlett O'Haras on a summer night. We must not play each other's rhythms!

3. I'm worried to death over the first act. I'm switching off some vital connection. I'm fighting something. I don't know what or why.

4. If I'm 25 in 1947, I spent my late teens and early twenties during WW2. What was that like? (Must go to the library and do research.) Born, bred, and lived until I was 18 in Mississippi. During the war years! What was that like? I must have been very poor. (Books of photographs of the period) Belle Reve, our family house, white columns. . . . (I can see it.) Class. Fallen aristocracy. (That's clear enough.)

Question: Why do I leave Blanche behind to deal with everything herself?

Answer: Maybe older sisters stay to take care of the parents; younger sisters run off to have their own lives. The narcissism of youth.

Question: What did I do in New Orleans 'til I met Stanley? Doesn't say.

Answer: I'll make that up.

Kay

Diary,

Personal confessions of an insecure actress: I've never submitted like Stella has. I've never found it fun or exciting to be slapped around, had my possessions thrown out the window, and to want more. I cannot relate to that kind of love. I've never been pregnant. Big fact and factor of the role. Just realized. My character's conflict! I am torn between loyalty to my husband and loyalty to my sister. (That helps. Makes me feel more active!) My loyalty to both puts me smack in the middle. Stella is who Stanley and Blanche are fighting over. (Good, I like that.) It's such a lovely fantasy: everyone fighting over me. Except it's a nightmare for Stella: She wants to make everyone happy and cannot.

Objective: I Want to Make Everyone Happy.

> 1. What do I want for myself? *No conflict, everyone happy.*
> 2. What do I get? *Conflict, conflict, conflict, and no one's happy.*

Kay

Diary,
Before we began the first act this morning it dawned on me: "I (Stella) have everything I want." Some characters never get what they want, and here is Stella, who has exactly what she wants at the start of the play: a husband who is crazy about her and a child inside her. When the play starts I am (figuratively) pregnant with happiness, happy to see Stanley and enjoying his crass jokes . . . and I am happy to see Blanche. My sister is here, my husband, my child, my world is complete. I must constantly remind myself:

> 1. Listen to what is being said.
> 2. Observe everyone.
> 3. Stay in the moment.

Remember when I'm playing with Blanche: She's the complicated one, she hides, dodges, zigzags; don't be afraid to be less interesting. This is not a play about two neurotic women!!!!!!!!!!!!!!!!! (*One will do.*)
I still hate the same thing about my character: her submission.
I'm a rag doll around Stanley; I sit on his lap and cry (like a jerk). And Blanche, rather cuttingly, suggests, "I guess that is what is meant by being in love . . ."
Kay

Diary,

Good rehearsal today. Was able to get much of the first scene to work. My head is in the right place, and May is a wonderful Blanche. I feel we are playing a sonata together . . . she the violin, me the piano. Except! May wants to come over and help me cue her. She's already done the part, but I think this is her way of weighing me down the way Blanche does with endless favors and becoming totally dependent on me. I hate actors who do that! They ought to keep their lives and their roles separate. . . . *Speaking of which, get this! Marvin, the actor, playing Stanley, the great unwashed.* Well, the director was giving notes, and she sniffs and says in her British way, "Heavens, it smells horrid in here!" And it's Stanley! She turns down her nose in his direction and says, "Stanley, did you step in something?" And Marvin says, "Sony, I was trying things without deodorant," and the director says, "Did you think that would improve your performance, darling?" And she looks at me and says, "Kay, darling, talk to Marvin. I don't know what you American actors think you're doing!" Marvin told me he thought Stanley Kowalski wouldn't wear deodorant, and I told him Stanley, for all his colorful crudity, is not antisocial! So Marvin says, why don't you buy me some? The kind Stella would like? Where will it end! He'll be knocking on my door in the middle of the night soon. Actors!

Kay

Diary,

Thought of Blanche's lines in the beginning of the play:

". . . they told me to take a streetcar named Desire, and then transfer to one called Cemeteries and ride six blocks and get off at Elysian Fields!" Elysian Fields is heaven! Does Blanche disrupt heaven?

These images of Tennessee's . . . especially the images in the play about "the heart" . . . the truth reveals the human heart in all its mystery, confusion, beauty, despair, and longing. Blanche, Stanley, and I must play together like this crazed string trio, instinctively, connected to each other's heart . . .

Kay

Diary,

I know scene three is powerful and beautiful. And all I'm doing is faking it. During Stanley's card game, Blanche and I are having fun, listening to the radio. He tears in the room, snatches the radio and throws it out the window. I order his friends out, he chases me out of the house, hits me a few times, and I run up to Eunice's. He cries out his famous *"Stella! Stella,* sweetheart! *Stella! Stell-Lahhhhhhh!"* Then we have the following 1940s ballet, which I cannot for the life of me relate to. *(The low-tone clarinet moans. The door upstairs opens again. Stella slips down the rickety stairs in her robe. Her eyes are glistening with tears, and her hair loose about her throat and shoulders. They stare at each other. They then come together with low, animal moans. He falls to his knees on the steps and presses his face to her belly, curving a little with maternity. Her eyes go blind with tenderness as she catches his head and raises him level with her. He snatches the screen door open and lifts her off her feet and bears her into the dark flat.)*

And the ending . . . when they are taking Blanche away . . . "Oh, God, what have I done to my sister?" And I cry after her, "Blanche! Blanche! Blanche!" I am left alone with Stanley. The stage directions read: "She sobs with inhuman abandon. There is something luxurious in her complete surrender to crying. . . ."

Why Am I Always Surrendering?

Then the hard part,

Stanley: *(kneels beside her and his fingers find the opening of her blouse)*
Now, now, love. Now, love . . .

I cannot submit to the submissiveness of the character.

Every time Marvin and I go into one of our passionate holds he whispers to me, "You're fighting it, baby, stop fighting!" I fight it tooth and nail. But I'm an actress, I'm supposed to be able to turn the character's emotions on and keep my own out of the way.

I must solve this problem.

Kay

Diary,
Truth time
I'm afraid of those feelings of powerlessness that control Stella—I am afraid of that side of myself. Not being in control, being weak, caving in to this man. *Except . . .*

Just very possibly I'm looking at Stella upside down. Maybe Stella is the one who controls Stanley through sex and desire. Maybe that's the dynamic I'm looking for to turn me on to Stella. After all, it is really Stanley who submits to me each time. He whines and cries and goes down on his knees and puts his head in my bosom.

I do have control in the situation.

I must look on our situation now not as my submitting to his desires as much as his giving me what I want.

What I have been unable to play has been "I want to submit." Well, damn it, I don't want to submit.

I'm going to try "I want him to pleasure me because he's been naughty, he's been cruel, he's made me suffer. We need each other's loving." (Goodness knows, Stella loves him to death.)

Yes, yes, I have to take all this out of the negative and put it in the positive. Suddenly Marvin is very attractive. I must make this happen onstage, though, not only in my head.
Kay

Diary,
Have thrown myself into Stella—totally committed to every part of it now. The director says my scenes with Stanley are shamelessly erotic for a pregnant woman. But she meant this as a compliment. I love controlling Marvin in those moments. I love to make him beg and to take my own sweet time to mother the bad boy back until he becomes my man again. I'm having fun at the outrageousness of displaying the sensual side of myself. I am becoming:

mother, lover
mother, wife
wife, lover
sister
Stella

I'm beginning to love this part.
Kay

Diary,

We are in dress/techs and will open soon, and this is my last entry for a while. Things are working well, and I just need to write what I've experienced and learned on the way to finding this character:

1. Ceaseless reading of the script and trying to catch the inspiration within the writing
2. Finding my character's music, which is quite different from my sister's and my husband's (both of which are distinctly different from each other as well)
3. Locating where my character fits in: She is the center of the conflict, being torn in two every moment
4. Confronting my fears as an actress:

   Fear of exposing certain levels of desire
   Fear of my character coming off stupid and a sponge
   Fear of being vulnerable

5. Taking the time to face the things I have to do in the text but am not able to relate to. Tearing down those barriers and putting my tasks in the positive: I am not surrendering to him, I am controlling him. If I surrender, it's because I want to. If I want to, it's because I love him.
6. Concentrating on my character's love of her husband. He is her life force:
   She is not intimidated sexually by him.
   She has as much power as he does in the marriage.
7. Listening
8. Getting a through-line of intentions. Such as: I want to make everyone happy.
9. I must remember that confronting the truth is staggering. It tears Blanche apart, leaves her without a vestige of illusion except to retreat from all truth through madness. Recognizing what part Stella has played in that area of the story.
10. Knowing I am not the kind of actor who has to become the character offstage: I do not have to go to the extremes May and Marvin do by bringing their onstage lives off.

11. Trusting myself to let go, to experience, to open up . . . trusting that when I do, I'm a pretty good actress.
12. Talking to you, diary.

Kay

Conclusions

Shortly after playing Stella, the actress landed another role. She went back to her diary and reread what she had written. In order to avoid some of the problems she had had in *Streetcar* she summarized what she had learned from the experience:

1. Resist prejudging the role (such as: my character is "not interesting" and so on).
2. A director who demands that you bring something to her is a good challenge. It was frightening at first, but it gave me a good sense of my own creativity.
3. Researching the role in the library in terms of photographs of the South, post-Depression literature, and the life of the author was very helpful. Reading Tennessee Williams's poems and prose opened my imagination to his world.
4. Always stay in the moment: I do this by listening, by finding an inner monologue, and keeping my impulses available to me at all times.
5. Think in opposites when I get stuck. If I think I'm submitting and that bothers me, I should think, "I'm not submitting; I'm making the other person submit."
6. Keep enjoying the process and my own ability to solve problems.

PUTTING IT TOGETHER (2)

An actor lands a role and begins his work. He familiarizes himself with the role, and as he does he sees various problems looming ahead and begins to wonder how he's going to solve them.

We have seen the usefulness of imagining an interview with your character. And keeping a diary as a way of verbalizing problems works as an important tool. It is essential that the artist keep questioning himself. You have to learn how to ask questions about the work and yourself in the work because every role is a puzzle to be solved. And in many ways you are the puzzle as well as the solution. Sometimes the way to answer questions is to ask more questions:

1. How am I going to use myself in this role?
2. Do I know enough about myself to relate to this character's experience?
3. What areas will be hard to play?
4. Will this role be easy for me?
5. What were my mistakes the last time out?
6. When I explore a role do I get lazy and too dependent on others?
7. Do I take enough responsibility for my performance?

AN ACTOR INTERVIEWS HIMSELF

The actor is about to begin rehearsal playing the role of Biff in Arthur Miller's *Death of a Salesman*.

Q: What are the problems you face as you begin work?
A: Here I am about to play Biff in *Death of a Salesman*, but he and I are very different people.

147

1. Biff is thirty-four. I'm ten years younger.
2. Biff's life is wrapped up with his father, and my father died when I was very young.
3. Biff has a brother, Happy, who is two years younger. I have an older sister.
4. Biff was brought up in the city and longs to live in the country. I live in the country and can't wait to live in a big city.
5. Biff and his brother have had lots of women, and I've been with the same girl since high school.

On top of all that, the really big problems are:

1. Because of the time factor in the play, I have to capture two Biffs: Biff as a high school athlete who adored his father and thought the world was made for him to conquer and Biff the thirty-four-year-old man struggling with what he didn't become, with what he wants now. There was Biff the young son who idolized his father, and Biff the mature man who has no more illusions about him.
2. Because I am the central force inside my father's mind, I must live up to that, shouldn't I? This great Greek god/hero/athlete/son. I should seem to be that—not only to the other characters, but to the audience as well. Otherwise, if I don't live up to that onstage the audience will think Willy is nuts to begin with.

How do I solve this?

Q: Let's take problems 1 through 5. What can you do?
A: Rely on my imagination to solve those differences between Biff and me.
Q: What about problems 6 and 7? Where do you start?

A: After pure inspiration I never know. Rehearsals begin next
week. It's my first paying job as an actor, and it means
everything to me.

Q: Can the actor who's playing your father help you? Can
you relate to him in ways that Biff does?

A: I called him last week, and we went for coffee. I made the
mistake of asking him if he had any advice for me, and he
said, "Yes. Give me my cues exactly as written and never
upstage me!"

What can I do when I'm playing a character whose life experience is almost the opposite of my own?

Q: How important is it to have had the same life experience
as the character? After all, how many of us have lived in a
castle at Elsinore, had our father visit us as a ghost, and
spend all our time contemplating murder?

A: I like bringing characters I play close to me. I think Biff is
a tremendous character, and I understand him completely.

Q: So why don't you learn the lines, give the cues exactly,
don't upstage anyone, and try not bumping into the
furniture?

A: I have too much respect for the audience to do that. I'm
going to be on the stage, in front of people who have paid
to see me. I want my work to be good. I don't want them
to walk out saying, "The guy playing Biff, wasn't he mis-
cast? He ruined one of the great masterpieces of the
American theatre!"

Q: I think these anxieties happen to you whenever you
haven't done quite enough work on the script. True?

A: True.

Q: Deal with the *universals* of the play: the things that are
eternal, the things all of us have gone through, one way
or the other.

No matter when it was written, who the people are, what style the performance is, the audience should be able to say, "Yes, I know what that is like, I've been there." Right?

A: I never know how to start.

I have to calm down, try to relax, and enter the play, or I'll have a good case of stage fright even before we begin.

Q: Close your eyes, Billy. Relax.

A: I'm relaxed; now what?

Q: *Death of a Salesman.* What do you feel? No intellectualizing, please, just a gut feeling. Where do you find your feelings going?

A: To the play. To the words, the mood, the characters moving in and out.

Q: How does the play make you feel?

A: Tense. The play is full of unremitting tension and conflict.

Q: What is the high point of the play as far as you're concerned—the biggest moment? I mean where is your character's Mount Everest?

A: Toward the end when I try to strip the delusions from my father's eyes and show him the truth. Maybe this is where I should begin to work on Biff: this scene, this stripping down, this unmasking. This is where Biff wants to be from the beginning of the play. His objective: to show his father who he, Biff, is. Or put another way, his objective is: He wants to face his own identity. He wants to tell it like it is, but his obstacle has always been that his father won't let him.

Q: So begin at the end.

A: You think? But I'm afraid that if I do that, I'll overload everything along the way. I'll tip the ending at the beginning.

Do I understand my character's story?

Q: Stop editing yourself before you've begun. Talk about your character. What do you know?

A: Background of my character: As a kid, until the end of high school I adored my father, Willy Loman. He lived for me and my brother, Happy. I was a football star in high school and had three scholarships to go to college. I was like one of these child prodigies who is brilliant at an instrument, whom great things are expected of, but who never develops further. My father filled me with how successful I was going to be. His credo was that I could really make anything I wanted of myself as long as I was liked. As long as I was popular, had the admiration of others, won that game, I'd make it in life.

I became something quite different.

The journey I take in the play is the journey of becoming who I really am.

Facts that cropped up in my character, such as academic laziness, thinking I could beat the system by working my way around it, problems with stealing—these were overlooked by my father. What were defects of character were viewed by Willy as assets. I had been warned I would not graduate from high school if I failed math. Both my father and I were too arrogant to heed the warning, and when I failed, my chances of going to college collapsed. I was distraught and confused and traveled up to Boston to talk to my father, who was up there on a business trip. He would counsel me, help me, make the disappointment go away. I needed him more than ever. I discovered him in his hotel room with another woman. When she left, he gave her new nylon stockings that he had promised my mother. I never forgave him.

It was the end of my hero worship of my father.

My father and I never talked about the incident.

I left home, went out west, came back home, left again. Always unable to settle into anything. My father thought that because I would not turn into the man he dreamed of I was "spiting" him. Spiting him! I wanted to punish him for betraying my mother with other women.

I'd always been physical and loved the outdoors, but so far this hasn't translated into a living. I come home once again, talk myself into a harebrained scheme of raising money to start a business from a man who doesn't remember me. I end up stealing his fountain pen.

In my last scene with my father I unleash the truth:

Biff: Why am I trying to become what I don't want to be? What am I doing in an office building making a contemptuous, begging fool of myself, when all I want is out there, waiting for me the minute I say I know who I am! Why can't I say that, Willy!

Willy: The door of your life is wide open!

Biff: Pop! I'm a dime a dozen and so are you!

Willy: I am not a dime a dozen! I am Willy Loman, and you are Biff Loman!

Biff: I'm one dollar an hour, Willy! I tried seven states and couldn't raise it. A buck an hour, do you gather my meaning? I am not a leader of men, Willy, and neither are you, you were never anything but a hard-working drummer who landed in the ash can like all the rest of them! I'm not bringing home any prizes any more and you're going to stop waiting for me to bring them home!

Willy: You vengeful, spiteful mutt! (*Biff grabs him and pulls him around, shaking him*)

Biff: Pop, I'm nothing, I'm nothing, Pop! Can't you understand that? There's no spite in it any more. I'm just what I am, that's all . . . (*He breaks down sobbing holds on to Willy, who takes him in his arms, comforting*)

Willy: What're you doing? What're you doing? Why is he crying?

Biff: Will you let me go, for Christ's sake? Will you take that phony dream and burn it before something happens? (*Struggling to contain himself he pulls away and moves to stairs*) I'll go in the morning. Put him . . . put him to bed.

Do I have anything in common with the character?

Q: Ever fought for your identity in your own life?

A: Of course, I have.

Q: Then that's the universal I was talking about. What was it in your case?

A: None of your business.

Q: You don't want to tell me?

A: That's right.

Q: But it's something you realize you can use in the part?

A: That's right.

Q: You think actors have secrets they won't tell even themselves?

A: I know what it is to please a parent. I know what it is not to be who your parent thinks you are. And worse still . . .

Q: What?

A: In all my struggles to be an actor so far, I may have to face the truth that I may not end up a movie star. I may not have the important career you are supposed to have to be a success in this country.

Q: Does that bother you?

A: It bothers me to think I can accept the possibility, but my family can't. Like Biff. He wants his father to accept him for who he really is. Not all of us want to be overachievers in the material sense. So does that make us worthless?

Q: Biff's kind of an artist.

A: Exactly. He's an artist without an art form. He wants to live life on his own terms once and for all. And that takes a lot of guts he's never quite had. Convictions, with finally enough courage.

Q: In the last scene he's found the courage.

A: He's been driven to his courage. He peels off the layers of lies and gets to the truth. He tells it to Willy like it is!

Q: That ever happen to you?

A: My mother thinks I'm going to be a big-time actor. It puts a lot of pressure on me. I'm not going to be anything like that. I don't have the opportunities, nor do I have the kind of blind faith in myself to make me a star. I'd like to be a good professional actor.

Q: Why don't you tell her?

A: It would be too painful.

Q: You think it's not painful for Biff?

A: You know, that's an interesting point I never thought of. Telling his father off, as much as he's suppressed it and has longed to do it, must tear his guts out. It's not an easy thing to do.

Q: Why isn't it easy? Why doesn't he just tell his old man the truth?

A: Because he loves the old fool, that's why. His conflict: He wants to tell him the truth, but he doesn't want to hurt him. I could never talk to my mother that way.

I see what's at stake.

Q: You see what is at stake?

A: At stake . . . yes! Destroying my mother is too high a cost.

Q: So then it's not just a lot of yelling and ranting at
Willy.

A: Yelling is easy. There is nothing in the scene that should
be easy for Biff or the actor.

Q: Biff confesses, "I just am what I am, that's all . . ."

A: Declares his identity once and for all.

Q: Breaks down, sobbing.

A: Admitting to his father that he is nothing.

Q: Yes, but does that tear the blinders from Willy's eyes?

A: Not at all. After I admit that, after I leave, after he
sees that I love him, he says, "That boy is going to
be magnificent." Deluded 'til the end. He will never
see the truth.

Q: Back to what is at stake.

A: I'm all my mother has in her life. How could I do such
a thing to her? Yet I can imagine it would be much like
what Biff does to Willy. I pay for this truth telling with
a lot of pain and the possibility of driving my parent over
the edge.

Q: So your sobbing in the scene . . .

I must avoid easy choices.

A: I have to earn all the tears. They can't be there as theatrical
effect or because I want to make the audience cry and feel
sorry for me. I'm crying because I'm letting Willy down.
I break his heart.

Q: What about the other Biff? The idealist, the opportunist,
the golden boy.

A: I was my mother's golden boy. Still am. The obstacle to
getting what I really want is that half the time, deep
inside, as much as I know it's not true, I still want to think
I am her golden boy. I still get suckered in to that ridiculous dream world of my parents.

Q: Have you ever stolen anything?
A: No, but I've had the impulse at times to take things.

Tell the truth, keep relating to Biff, keep understanding his needs.

Q: Can you explain it?
A: I don't know where it comes from, but it has been
there—I've seen things I've been fascinated with,
wanted to take. Biff gets this overwhelming compulsion
to have the pen. He takes it and rationalizes the theft
later.
Q: This compulsion to steal . . .
A: Goes right along with his compulsion to confess who and
what he is. Biff, above all, wants to be an honest man.
Honesty will free him.
Q: What does he really want in life?
A: To be happy.
Q: You could say that about any character. We all want to be
happy.
A: It's how we're going about getting that happiness
that's interesting. Biff does not believe his father
is honest. He caught him with another woman.
Whenever Biff is around his parents, he finds
himself lying because they don't want to hear
the truth.
Q: They want to hear him lie?
A: They want to hear that he is working on things, believing
in things, doing things they consider useful toward
becoming a success.
Q: Do you lie?
A: We all lie to our parents: in order to make them happy,
I guess. Sometimes.
Q: I thought you said Biff wants to be happy.

A: He does. The price he has to pay to make his parents happy is making himself miserable. He knows that if he made himself happy by telling the truth, they'd be crushed. Finally he can't stand it anymore. Finally what becomes at stake is his manhood! Thirty-four years old and he has debased himself by performing the pettiest of thefts—and he must break from this terrible cycle once and for all.

Q: Wage war and end the conflict.

A: It gets to be life or death. You or me. I survive or you survive. In that kind of battle I am the one who will survive. At least that's what my character thinks.

Q: Is Biff's age still bothering you?

A: Less and less. The physical side of his character might help me a great deal. I'm going to work out all those old football moves. Take a ball to rehearsal. Get into those fantasies of playing the big game. High-energy moves, tackles, victory. Get back to the rhythm and dynamics of high school kids.

And I want to observe older guys now. Watch them playing. See how their bodies have changed. How it's not so easy. If I concentrate on the physical, really make something of it, I can capture an essence of the two Biffs.

Q: And all Biff's women?

A: I bet it's all a bluff, come to think of it. He's a loner. He stands in the middle of a cheering crowd, feeling totally alone.

Hey, that's a good image, I think I'll use it! It just hit me like a ton of bricks.

Q: What?

A: Imagine if I caught Mom in a hotel room with a man when I was in high school.

Q: What would you feel?

A: Fear. Lost. Betrayed. Crazy—angry at everything.

I know more than I thought I knew.

Q: How would you sum up?
A: It's very helpful to articulate the differences between me and the character.

1. Look to see if there is a common ground between us.
2. If I think there aren't similarities, I should look again. If the play represents a universal experience, there's a good chance I will have shared something about it.
3. Understand the character's progression. In this case, from high school to the present (he's now thirty-four). Understand who he was, what he's failed to become.
4. Do I really have a way of working as an actor? Always go back to basics:

   Respond to the play subjectively.
   Dig in to what the character is after.
   Understand the specifics of the story.

5. The play pivots on the truth. My character progresses from illusions to self-knowledge. I see I can work from the ending of the play, building toward it from the beginning, layer by layer. Seeing the full progression of the character is very exciting and more than challenging. The progression is the road my character takes. And although he does not always see this road or where he's going, the actor has to.
6. Use some of my personal secrets to understand the character: shared dreams of making it, of success. How people around me want me to become a big shot, when I know I'm not going to.
7. Always look to see what is at stake for my character so that I can generate what he wants *now*.

8. Keep thinking like an actor: in terms of how my character behaves and how I can use myself and my imagination to visualize that behavior.
9. When I feel I understand the life of the character, I begin to know I can play it.

Final Comment

Actors need to trust that they have a brain and to stop letting everyone else do the thinking for them. I seem to have gone from confusion, terror, and no confidence to utter inspiration.

EXTENDING YOUR RANGE

Developing techniques that enhance actors'
courage and enjoyment in performing:

- Comedy

- One-person shows, cabaret, and performance art

- Research projects: social issues and activists

13

|| ■ || ■ || ■ ||

COMEDY

The actor begins to experience the principles and practice of comedy toward the end of a training program or sometime during a career. Comedy is thought to be alternately too sophisticated to master or too irrelevant to teach. However, I have found it to be one of the cornerstones of an actor's development. In a perfect world, comedy should be taught side by side with autodrama, text, imagination, and character. Certain connoisseurs of comedy will look at that last sentence and object to "should be taught" because they don't believe that comedy can be taught.

SOME OBSERVATIONS ON COMEDY

My opinion that comedy needs to be integral to actor training, right from the beginning, is based on these observations:

1. Concentrating, listening, playing together, pursuing objectives via interesting actions, and staying inside the play and inside your character are elemental in any play, especially a comedy. Comedy often extends the actor's imagination as far as it can go.
2. A student who is at a loss doing naturalistic behavior, or a student who is fighting the process of that kind of work, whose responses are half-dead and turned off, who is unable to function may very well have a gift for another kind of work. And that work is tearing down the fourth wall and using the audience. This student may be able to flourish in comedy.
3. Quite a few actors suppress their native sense of humor because they believe they have to be "serious" on

the stage. Actors who are inherently funny but who try to be only serious are often very dull actors. They don't allow what's really inside of them to flow into the work.

Granted, this is a very large subject, and talking about comedy on paper is very much like people telling what they think is a hilarious story only to find that no one is laughing at it. Finally they'll say, "You had to be there." Comedy can be very technical. Some comedians talk about the principles of playing comedy as though they were rocket scientists: They love discussing the mathematical precision of split-second timing. What they forget when they tell you about the great way they timed a joke to get a laugh and how they waited just so long and got the next laugh, and so on, is that they are they! No one else's timing is yours. There are principles of playing comedy, there are fundamentals, there are rules; but you have to find a way that you, the actor, can navigate through these with your own personality and sensibility intact.

Exercises

1. Tell jokes to the group. Good jokes, awful jokes. Divide yourselves up into joke-telling teams. Play games in which the best jokes win or the worst ones win. In these days of political correctness it is probably wise to be sensitive in your choice of material unless the group determines otherwise.
2. Make the most outrageous entrance you can think of. How you come in, what you have on, what you say or don't say are up to you.
3. Surprise the group. Slip out and re-enter as someone else. Find a costume, use makeup as a completely outrageous disguise. See how long you can sustain this.
4. Do an autodrama. This time your life is a farce. Dig out the absurd aspects of what you have lived through. Take some of the more serious events and see what happens when you put a comic spin on them.

4. Do a serious scene you worked on recently and present it as a comedy. You can turn it into a parody, improvise the lines, play it like animals—anything goes.

5. Physicalize as much as possible. Rent some silent films. Observe how comedians like Charlie Chaplin and Buster Keaton used their bodies. Invent a silent character of your own. Using other members of the group make a live "silent" movie on stage.

6. Observe the people closest to you. Portray some of their more amusing characteristics.

7. Work with props. Try a comic piece of business with one prop. Perhaps an object that defies you. Try transforming one object into another: a towel into a baby, a telephone into a hand mike, and so on. Try drinking something while telling a joke in order to time the business with the line. Try telling the story of your day, using the props you encountered.

CONCENTRATION

In comedy, as an actor you are usually playing a character who is passionately pursuing an objective. But that pursuit becomes difficult because the audience keeps getting in the way of the actor's concentration. It's like you planned a trip in a small car for you and your family and suddenly there are several hundred people hanging on for the ride. You have to be aware of the audience as a performer and unaware of it as the character. Some typical questions:

How much attention do I pay to the audience?

You have to be fully concentrated on what you are playing. You have to be completely in the moment, playing with the other actors. At the same time you need to be attuned to the audience but not let them know you are. You always stay in character.

What is the fourth wall? Do I break it in comedy?

The fourth wall is the imaginary barrier between actors and audience. You can't break it, unless the play demands it, and then it can be broken only "in character." In plays in which the character comes down to talk to the audience, the concentration problem is greater. The audience response is unpredictable. Whether you play off the audience or not depends on the script. But no one wants to see the actor's "take" on the situation. Stay inside the story.

How do I keep my concentration when half my brain is focusing on getting the laugh, then listening to the audience to see when I can come in for the next line?

Stay in character. You do not want to appear to be manipulating members of the audience. It makes them uncomfortable. They become aware that you are soliciting them. Audiences, in that case, will laugh out of uneasiness just to make the performer happy. Or they'll get hostile when really pushed.

You can't be unaware of the audience, either. That's not being true to the play. Actors who are determined not to "play for laughs" are being irresponsible.

There are huge laughs in O'Neill's *Long Day's Journey into Night*. If you ignore them, you are cheating the audience out of necessary comic relief and yourself out of different colors in your portrayal.

What you learn only through experience is this: You must seem to be fully in character, but you must know where the laughs are and how to get them. The success or failure of the play depends on it.

How do I keep connected with the other actors?

It is often tempting to take solo flights during a comedy and to forget everyone else on the stage. A laugh is the result of everyone's work. The person delivering the punch line won't get a laugh without the successful delivery from the person who has the setup or the feed line.

Recently an actor said the following about playing comedy:

> *You have to learn to stop manipulating the audience . . . so you want a laugh here, fine. Frequently you get a laugh . . . sometimes the other*

person gets the laugh. It takes two people to get a laugh . . . sometimes it takes seven people to get a laugh.

PHYSICAL COMEDY

Someone once defined farce as "the relentless pursuit of an objective to the point of absurdity." That's a good definition not only of farce but also of most comedy. The objectives in classical comedy revolved around basic life needs: food, money, love, sex. The characters pursuing these objectives were the jealous lover, the innocent girl, the scheming friend, the cuckolded husband, the wacky doctor, and other types. The plots were built on disguises and mistaken identities and carried out by a very clever servant who was a combination contortionist, juggler, acrobat, and ringmaster. In the twentieth century, when the servant class in the United States began to diminish, this character became Everyman. He was always in hot water, but we liked him. He was an underdog, fighting the system, and everyone could identify with him. It's Charlie Chaplin, Buster Keaton, and, later, Lucille Ball. The objective is always achieved through a combination of will and body; in most cases, body.

Silent Films Are the Best Example of Physical Comedy

Example 1
Rent Buster Keaton's *The General.* It is a demonstration of playing actions and objectives through physical means. Keaton's character wants to rescue his sweetheart, who has been abducted by the Union army. He gets hold of a train and sets out to rescue her. Overcoming every physical obstacle imaginable, tireless and undaunted, he engineers his train to final victory.

1. The objective: to save his love
2. The actions: finding ways to take the train to its final destination

3. What's at stake: his woman, his manhood, and the honor of the South
4. Obstacles: everything

How is it done? Absolute concentration on what he is doing. He never telegraphs that he's being funny. He's not aware of his acrobatics or physical brilliance: He simply makes you feel he's an ordinary guy, fighting to get back what's rightfully his. As a matter of fact, Keaton is so serious that he makes you wonder if he knew he was making a comedy.

Example 2

Lucille Ball was a great physical clown. The high point of most *I Love Lucy* episodes was an extended piece of physical business. Among her many classic performances are "Lucy Does a TV Commercial" and "Lucy's Italian Movie." Both shows have certain similarities in their premise:

1. Lucy wants to do something that her husband, Ricky Ricardo, does not want. Her burning ambition is to be in show business.
2. She comes up with a scheme to get what she's after, but it backfires, and she gets into trouble.
3. Chaos reigns supreme as she turns everything upside down in the pursuit of her goal.

In the show about the TV commercial, she wants to do the commercial on her husband's show. He won't let her. He wants a professional actress. To prove to him that Lucy can be good at it, she guts the insides of their home television set, gets inside, and, when he comes home, she is where the picture tube would normally be, trying to do a commercial.

He refuses to hear of it. She is upset, won't talk to him, and still is plotting to get what she wants. (This is going back to "the relentless pursuit of an objective to the point of absurdity.") When the woman who is scheduled to do the commercial calls, Lucy tells her the part has been filled and shows up herself at the studio.

She fobs herself off as the spokesperson for the product and goes into a series of rehearsals with the director. Unbeknownst to Lucy, the product is 28 percent alcohol. We know it, she doesn't, and we wait for her to get drunk. Lucy never disappoints.

Slowly she gets more and more tipsy as she is asked to rehearse repeatedly. It is a great lesson in physical comedy. As she becomes more inebriated, she finds herself having a better time with the commercial; but everything becomes her obstacle. She can't pour the liquid into the spoon, she slops it onto the table, off the table, scoops it up, finally swigs it from the bottle, and crosses over to the section of the set where Ricky is live on camera and gets into the middle of his act. He is shocked and annoyed and frustrated. She is drunk and undaunted. He tries to throw her off, but she comes back, stumbles all over the place, and is finally carried off the set. It's complete anarchy. Lucy indulges all our fantasies of toppling institutions and creating chaos. At the same time that we are saying, "Oh, no" we are also saying, "I could never do that, but, Lucy, go for it!"

(The Italian movie episode contains Lucy's fight with another woman in a vat full of crushed grapes—a classic demonstration of physical comedy.)

Comic business is sometimes referred to as shtick, defined in the dictionary as "a comedian's stage routine." Physical shtick is oxygen to many actors. And you will notice in *Lucy* that the shtick often develops with a prop.

Research

The videos of Keaton, Chaplin, and Laurel and Hardy define "shtick" and the art of physical comedy. Monty Python is very good, but there much of the humor relies on camera tricks.

1. Observe your favorite comedians. Turn off the sound and just watch what they are doing. Steve Martin and Lily Tomlin are expert physical clowns. So are Tom Hanks and Eddie Murphy.

2. Observe people who are always getting into physical trouble: They break things all the time and always have some great physical objective, which they rarely achieve—like walking into the closet when they mean to go out the front door. Children are very useful to watch in this regard.

VERBAL COMEDY

Physical comedy is a language all its own. Verbal comedy uses words as its principal vehicle for laughter. There are plays and films that mix both. Physical comedy and verbal comedy are equally technical. The way you walk into a wall is as choreographed as the way you say a line, phrase a speech, time the jokes, and cue your partner. This isn't to say you can't improvise physical ideas before you turn them into a worked-out routine. You can. All the improvisation work that the actor explores in the preceding chapters can go on when dealing either with physicality or with text and language. But in comedy their parameters are set more specifically by the end of rehearsal—certainly by the end of previews. Because of the flow that the actors find working together in comedy, each performer has to stay within precise confines, or else the laughs won't be there anymore.

Here are a few problems you may have while playing verbal comedy:

1. Breath support
2. Ends of sentences
3. Phrasing
4. Timing
5. Conveying the meaning of the line

Let's look at the opening lines of Oscar Wilde's *The Importance of Being Earnest.*

Act 1. Scene: Morning—mom in Algernon's flat. The room is luxuriously and artistically furnished. The sound of a piano is heard in the adjoining room. Lane is arranging afternoon tea on the table and after the music has ceased, Algernon enters.

Algernon: Did you hear what I was playing, Lane?

　　Lane: I didn't think it polite to listen, sir.

Algernon: I'm sorry for that, for your sake. I don't play accurately— anyone can play accurately—but I play with wonderful expression. As far as the piano is concerned, sentiment is my forte. I keep science for Life.

　　Lane: Yes, sir.

You can see that in just the opening speeches Wilde sets his tone: a very witty comedy that twists and bends everything for its own comic convenience: "I didn't think it polite to listen, sir."

Depending on how the scene is set up, if Algie's playing is horrible enough, Lane's reactions can be very funny. In any event, his line, "I didn't think it polite to listen, sir," is the first verbal joke of the play. (Often young actors think jokes are low things that stand-ups and sitcoms stoop to. Jokes are a very legitimate part of any story. Jokes are defined as: "A thing said or done to excite laughter or amusement." They abound in Shakespeare, Chekhov, Strindberg, and so on.)

Invariably every joke has a feed line to it. This is the line that sets up and supports the joke. "Did you hear what I was playing, Lane?" is the feed line for Lane's joke. The joke is also referred to as a punch line, a laugh line, or a gag.

Of course, the actor playing Lane is completely in character, completely in the moment, and says the line with immense seriousness. He does not play it like a joke.

He might also get a laugh before the line by doing a "take." A "take" is a silent reaction to a line you just heard. It's as if to say, "Did you hear what I heard?" In vaudeville, the comic would be playing with his partner, and his take would be to the audience. Many laughs depend on the take. If I have the punch line, your reaction to it, or take, is what will get the laugh. In the case of *Earnest,* Lane stops whatever business he's doing and looks at his master in utter disbelief that Algie would think that he would listen, while we in the audience know that Lane has painfully heard the playing. Or the actor playing Lane can do his take in the direction of the audience, but not play that the audience is there—just do his take in its direction. It would probably get a better laugh. (Masters of the "take" include Jack Benny, Jackie Gleason, Whoopi Goldberg, and Billy Crystal.)

Algie's response, "I'm sorry for that, for your sake," is designed to be the "topper." A "topper" is a bigger laugh than the one immediately preceding it.

Breath Support

There is a tendency for the young actor to exhale, then to say the line. This causes the line to be said when there is no breath left to speak it, or the line to be said as the actor gulps out whatever is left in his lungs. Worse, the line is said as the actor is inhaling air—but not enough air to complete the line. There is a mistaken notion that in order to relax you should exhale and that this will release tension. Unfortunately, all this does is release the breath needed to say the line. Imagine a singer who had no breath to belt out the lyric, who sang only after inhaling, and you have the sound made by many actors.

Acting needs to be on the breath: You time the amount of breath you need to say the line, then say it as you are exhaling. For example, take in all the air you need to say the first line: "Did you hear what I was playing, Lane?" It's not a long line. You should be able to do it in one breath.

If you exhale first and do the line while you are inhaling, this will happen:

1. You will need to take a breath somewhere in the line.
2. You will run out of breath before you say "Lane."
3. You will drop the end of the sentence. If the end of the sentence is dropped on an important feed line, the actor who has the next line, which is the joke, will not get the laugh. You have killed the setup.

Phrasing

How do you read the line, "Did you hear what I was playing, Lane?"? Some actors will shriek, "He's giving me line readings!" Others will beg you, "Please give me a reading on that line so I can get the laugh." There are eight words to that line. Which words are stressed or emphasized? Or is the whole line thrown away, which means that nothing is stressed and that it's funniest just to toss it off?

Go Back to the Verbs Exercise

"hear"
"playing"

Slowly add on the other words.

"Did you hear what I was playing, Lane?"

It's not so much a question of stressing words or punching words as it is of putting an emphasis of feeling under them.

But Don't Forget "Lane"

You might get so involved with "Did you hear what I was play . . ." that you will drop "Lane." Wilde knew he needed "Lane" after "playing." "Playing" is not a strong word to end a sentence. Ending the sentence on "Lane" with its good, strong "aaayyyynnnnnnn" sound gives the line resonance. The line is built this way to help the actor.

Don't Forget Your Action

On another level you can examine Algie's line from the point of view of his action. Is he trying to get Lane to flatter him? Is he amusing himself with Lane? Does he believe that he plays inaccurately but with wonderful expression and that Lane would agree? *Either* try the line technically for a particular reading, then try playing the action, *or* play an action and see how the line falls.

Timing and Meaning

Timing begins when you realize you are on the stage with other actors. You work as a team. The give-and-take, the full awareness of each other, the playing off of each other, the always being there for each other like acrobats or musicians in a quartet—all these create timing that comes from the interplay of people performing together.

Exercise
The next time you go to a play make yourself aware of how the actors are delivering the lines. You might find the following problems:

1. Actors who are taking a long time on a line. Saying, "I want to get a pack of cigarettes" may take a full minute. The timing distorts the line's meaning. Timing and meaning go together. Distorted meaning implies:
   a. The actor doesn't know what the lines mean.
   b. The actor is playing what he believes to be dramatic effect, not content.
   c. The actor is so tense that his breath is not flowing.
2. At the same time, listen to how actors pick up their cues. That is, the time it takes for them to speak after the other actor finishes. How long should it take the actor playing Lane to say, "I didn't think it polite to listen, sir"? If he takes a very long time, he will not get the laugh because the audience will have forgotten the cue. If he rushes right in, it's jarring and uneasy.

Let's go to his action. If he has been disturbed by the playing and wants to cover up, he is being truly polite.

Play your intentions fully and see how they time out. Timing and action go together. If you fill the line with an intention and an emotional color, you will get the laugh (usually).

Beyond getting a laugh, how your character times, phrases, uses breath to speak, and articulates is largely who that character is. After the audience gets in tune with that, you can take it almost anywhere.

COMIC CHARACTERS

Comedies usually mix clowns and "straights." The straight is the workhorse of the show. He or she is in serious trouble and is the center of the story. Rosalind in *As You Like It* and Viola in *Twelfth Night* are examples. Instead of the clowns who are doing pratfalls and other comic routines, the straights are getting their laughs through wit, which is a high degree of language, wordplay, puns, and irony.

A clown can be easier than a straight to play. It is great fun to let out all the stops: funny noses, funny makeup, funny shoes and costumes, funny wigs, funny voices, and endless stage business. However, I suggest that you take some time to look before you leap into a "funny characterization," especially if you are an actor, not a comic. (Comics are people who tell jokes—Chris Rock, David Letterman, Joan Rivers, Jackie Mason. Comedians are actors who are funny when they are playing a role—Robin Williams, Jack Lemmon. Some comics have become actor/comedians: Woody Allen, Eddie Murphy, Ellen DeGeneres.)

BEHAVIOR

In addition to all the work that actors normally do, when playing a comedy you should take special care in observing your character's behavior for the following:

1. **Intensity of objective:** In comedy you have to be willing to turn the world upside down to get what you are after. Anarchy reigns supreme. Strong wants and actions have to be chosen.
2. **Conflict:** Make sure you are at cross-purposes with either the other characters, the social system, or the world. Your character is in the midst of a struggle. How he or she goes about it is what's funny.
3. **Tension:** Your character is in trouble, and something big is at stake. Funny as the play is, it must be life and death to you.

4. **Contrast:** Try to make sure your character is not blending into the scenery. You don't want to play someone else's shtick in the same show (unless it's funny). Contrasts in appearance, in behavior, in attitude generally work. Tall and short, fat and thin, fastidious and sloppy, fast and slow, and so on.

AUDIENCES

No two houses are the same. There are the so-called "hot" houses that are laughing before the curtain goes up and are ready for you to knock them dead. There are "tough" houses that are very difficult and won't laugh at anything. There are houses that start lukewarm and get hotter as the evening goes on. There are houses that you lose: They start great but die on you. There are houses that "should have stayed at home." There are houses that ate and drank too much before the show, houses that are worrying about the thunderstorm, or houses that loved you so much they didn't let you go, and so on.

The actor often misjudges the audience. If you're up there with funny materials, you want laughs. It's deadly without them. If the audience isn't laughing, or if you are not hearing the laughs that you got the night before, it doesn't mean that the audience is not fully enjoying itself. Very often seemingly "tough" houses that haven't responded during the show will give a very rousing ovation at the end. Their ovation is often more demonstrative than that of audiences that have laughed their heads off: It's just a different way of demonstrating enjoyment, which is on different levels for every house and every person in that house. I've heard audience members who didn't laugh once say, "That was the funniest show I ever saw." So maybe laughing out loud doesn't always indicate an audience's true feelings.

Some actors will do anything for a laugh. They will break the conventions of the material, practically talk to the audience, step outside the moment, and unleash their hostility on an audience that isn't finding them funny enough. Some will walk on their ankles and fall on their backsides to get that laugh. Seemingly reasonable men and women have been reduced to such efforts publicly. They are hard to play with—and all too easy to turn into.

■ ‖ ■ ‖ ■ ‖ ■ ‖ ■ ‖ ■ ‖ ■ ‖ ■ ‖ ■ ‖ ■ ‖ ■ ‖ ■ ‖ ■ ‖ ■ ‖ ■

FREQUENTLY ASKED QUESTIONS

Q: Why are some actors driven to such excess in comedy?

A: It's outside the realm of this book to explore why actors want to perform and what rewards they expect. Playing comedy can easily get out of control if certain questions are not answered from the beginning:

1. What reality are we playing in? Are we "real" people or cartoons? Are we stylized, and if so, how?

2. How funny do we want to be? Is this a knockabout farce or a very sophisticated comedy of manners?

3. How far are we going, and are we all going to the same place together? Does anything go to get a laugh, or do some of us have other responsibilities in this show, such as carrying the plot or creating the dramatic tension?

4. Who's supposed to get the laughs? All of us, some of us? Are we tolerating greedy actors who think they're the only ones who should get the laughs?

Q: What about the process of relating to the character—is it the same as for a serious play?

A: It should be. Even if you put on masks and work within highly stylized movement, you have to take the time to find the comic truth of the piece. It will be a universal truth that both the audience and the actor can relate to. The truth in comedy is a highly distilled essence, like a precious elixir. Inside this elixir is the entire human situation in all its forms.

Q: Is it true that an objective reading of the text is very important in comedy?

A: Very. The actor has to be aware of the comment that the piece is making about the human condition.

Q: I need to know more about concentration when I'm playing comedy. How do I stay inside the play as the character and be attuned to the audience response at the same time?

A: There are certain questions that only the actor can answer by experience. Stay in character, play your intentions, work to talk and to listen to the other players on the stage, and let yourself act inside the situation. If the audience is laughing, their concentration, their absorption of the moment will force you to stay inside the play. One false move and you'll break the link between you—it's that delicate.

Q: You seem to indicate that physical comedy has to be choreographed. How choreographed?

A: Completely choreographed. Uncontrolled energy on the stage is a dangerous weapon. All physical business should be worked out in terms of practicality and safety. Never do anything onstage because of peer pressure, misplaced pride, or vanity. Either work it out fully or don't do it.

Q: Isn't "faster and funnier" a rule in comedy?

A: Yes, and it's a completely stupid one. Faster is not funnier. Faster is often slower because the less you vary the rhythm, the more tedious its effect. Most good laughs come out of dramatic tension: those moments that have the audience on the edge of its seats, moments that have been carefully built into the story as releases and surprises.

Q: If you go too fast you're liable to miss twists, reversals, and unexpected turns?

A: That's right. You gloss over the details of the story and the audience's fun at watching your character behave within the story.

---

continued on page 178

continued from page 177

Q: After you set a routine, can't you change it in performance?

A: Not unless everyone involved gets to fully rehearse the changes.

Q: What about changes of line readings and timing during a performance?

A: Actors are always fiddling with their readings, always trying something in performance. But because these little "improvements" affect everyone onstage, you ought to let everyone know beforehand what you want to try. If another actor is expecting the cue line to land in a certain way, you will throw him way off. He's like a catcher in an aerial act: If you spin at him in a different way, he can only let you drop to the net, revealing your mistake and ineptitude to the audience.

Q: How can I develop skills in verbal comedy?

A: Hopefully you have a good ear. If you do, you've won half the battle. If you can hear it on the page, you can play it.

Again, develop your:
Breath support
Resonance
Articulation
Dialect skills
Reading aloud
Observation of people
Storytelling abilities
Appreciation of language

Q: I worry that it's all very technical and that I'll become . . .

A: A technical actor? All acting is technical, let's not fool ourselves. If you are talking about being intuitive, inspired, instinctive—yes, there is all of that. But those have to be transformed into stage technique as well.

Q: Can comedy be taught?
A: If it can be learned, it can be taught. In the end, it will be taught by yourself through your own experience.

ONE-PERSON SHOWS, CABARET, PERFORMANCE ART, RESEARCH PROJECTS

Many autodramas have been the genesis of one-person shows, cabarets, and performance art. After actors get into the swing of developing and performing their own theatrical pieces, they realize that the possibilities are endless. Daring to perform a piece of theatre of your own invention takes a great deal of actor's courage, which you'll always need plenty of. It also forces you to take charge of yourself onstage: You have to organize your show from top to bottom and use everything you know or think you know or to quickly remember what you forgot.

It also empowers the actor, who is not dependent on:

> Being cast. He has cast himself.
> Searching for a good script. He has put the material together himself.
> Being simpatico with the director. He's the director.
> Having conflicts with rehearsal. It's all on his time.
> Being kicked out of the theatre. He can play it anywhere.

BEGINNING

There are many ways to start. Here are a few:

> 1. The actor will decide to develop his autobiographical ten minutes into a half-hour piece. Thirty minutes is a very long time to hold the stage alone. It requires a

lot of interesting material and will take months to evolve. But it's a good assignment because it demands a great deal of thinking on the actor's part, as well as learning the trial-and-error process of what works and what doesn't.

2. The actor is assigned "free ten minutes" in which to perform anything he or she desires. This exercise has been the core of several performance pieces that are a combination of the actor's life, fantasy, and written material. One woman developed a project based on her response to images that haunted her in some of Anne Sexton's poems.

3. A group of actors will want to work together on something because they enjoy the chemistry that happens between them onstage. Recently three women were looking through plays and could find nothing of interest. Each was working part time as a waitress. One of the actresses did a ten-minute piece about her job. The other two followed suit. Finally they decided to combine their pieces and developed an ensemble event called *The Working Actor.*

THE ONE-PERSON SHOW

Developing the Idea

If you have an idea, consider presenting only ten minutes of it first. If you don't have ten minutes, try five. Don't worry about not having the piece totally worked out. Bring in rough ideas, sketches, impulses. It's not important that you know where you are going, just get your ideas out there. One fellow had an impulse to dramatize his life as an Italian Catholic growing up in an eastern coast city. He brought in scenes in which he played the local pizza baker, his parish priest, the biology teacher who taught his class sex education, his grandfather. Eventually he shaped fifteen minutes of it. After performing it several times and listening to feedback, he built a thirty-minute show that was very funny and very engaging.

Other Examples

A young woman worked her way through college by being a waitress in a topless night club. She began work on her one-person show by doing some character sketches of the dancers as they came offstage into the dressing room. Somehow she never struck the right tone and almost gave up on the idea when we asked her to show us what she did in the club. She acted out taking orders for drinks and bringing them over to the men. Then, she went on to tell us how she made miserable tips until she learned that the customers loved dumb girls, and the dumber she became— such as not remembering any of the orders, being ditsy and helpless—the better her tips got. The story of herself as the waitress gave her a good ten minutes to enact. She needed twenty more.

She developed a character based on one of the girls at the club—a dancer who was angry, frustrated, confused, and who hated her work. She just wanted to take cocaine, was totally messed up about men, about life, about everything. The actress now had twenty minutes.

Inevitably, the only other character to explore in this club was a typical man who frequented such a place. The actress put on a suit and tie and played a man watching the girls and verbalized an inner monologue going on in his mind. It was hair-raisingly accurate. She had thirty minutes of very good theatre.

A former football player developed a show about his high school and college athletic career. At first it was very much about the ritual of putting on his uniform, having the desire to win, and being part of the mythos of the game.

After he presented the first ten minutes, he realized he was avoiding what he really wanted to present. He never scored a touchdown in his entire career; he just systematically did damage to other players. What he really wanted to portray was the desire to hurt other players. He then created, from several guys he knew, a composite of one brute of a man who was boorish, outrageously coarse, and whose idea of a party was harassing and abusing women. For the audience, the piece was an insight into a side of the sport that is not talked about very much: sadism.

A frequently asked question is "Is there some rule of thumb about doing one-person shows?" The only answer I can give is that they work best when the actor takes the audience down paths that it hasn't been down before, into unknown territories: what the women are really going through in a topless club, what the football player really wants in the tackle, and so on.

CABARET

Cabaret is a challenge for any group, from freshmen to show business veterans: If you sing, dance, play an instrument, tell stories, like comic routines and sketches, have an idea of how messed up the world is and really would like to straighten it out, put together a cabaret. Use masks, use puppets, use video or gadgets. Use a stage. If a stage isn't available, use a room. If a room isn't available, do it outdoors. Don't let real estate stop you. And don't be stopped by narrow definitions of cabaret. Restaurant service need not be available, and the fare does not have to be musical. Cabaret is an entertainment that can be as structured or as unstructured as the participants like. It's an evening that has been pulled together by its diversity. It can be timely and pertinent in terms of a message it wants to get across, or it can have no message at all. It's fundamentally about performing, and anything goes.

Examples

One fellow, whose acting problem had been a lack of true involvement, told us a story of his escapades in the navy while stationed in the Philippines. The story was very funny and outrageous, and although I had a bias against stand-up because it is solo playing, the story relaxed the actor in a way we hadn't seen before. He liked getting laughs and was able to connect to an exhi-bitionist side of himself.

When he had to act someone else's material he was always looking at himself self-consciously. When he was himself, or the side of himself he knew we'd enjoy, he flourished. Every week for the next ten weeks we got fifteen minutes of "Dave in the Navy." The stories got better and better. I couldn't believe they all were true, but he insisted they were. After a while I wondered if he just imagined they were true. He went from an artless storyteller to a skillful raconteur. He slipped in his jokes, knew how to build to his tension, and was learning how to be a savvy performer of his own material. He was urged to do other things as well, but he insisted he couldn't because he had many other stories to tell.

The following year I saw him in a play and told him what a long way I thought he had come. He was in the moment, he was not looking at himself, his concentration was excellent, and he seemed to be enjoying himself up there.

He said, "Thanks to those damned navy stories you made me do!"

Anna, a shy young woman from the Philippines, took courage from Navy Dave. She had been inward, shy, and hated the idea of cabaret. She said she was an actress and had no sense of invention. One day she put herself on the list of work to be shown.

We were in the theatre. The lights went down, and we heard Tchaikovsky's *Swan Lake* in the darkness. As the stage lights came up, we saw Anna curled up like the dying swan. The music built, and she slowly raised her head, fluttered her arms, and rose. Seeing her in a tutu was funny enough, but when she stood she was wearing huge rubber frog feet, the kind used in scuba diving. She proceeded to dance, completely straight-faced, to the music: pirouetting, leaping with the frog feet on. Later she performed it with great success at several public cabarets.

Working with a particular actor in a scene-study class was diffi-cult. All he wanted to do was perform. He refused to find a process for himself. His concentration was always on the audience. He could not be broken of this habit.

He developed a sketch doing a variation on Sherlock Holmes that was a bawdy, unpredictable, homoerotic detective story of his own invention. His imagination, which had been locked up in some corner of his rigid mind for years, poured out. Suddenly he was a very interesting actor. He was concentrating on his work and not on the audience. I never thought him capable of this. And it took a sketch to do it. I think that having a fourth wall was intolerable to him. That invisible wall made him want to take the audience's pulse every ten seconds: "Are you watching me? Do you love me?" When he was doing cabaret, there was no wall; he could look at us if he wanted to. But he didn't want to, because he knew he could. He was fully at ease. It was as if we were suddenly the light shining on him, and he no longer had to be afraid of the dark.

A cabaret sketch can also be worked out by an entire group. I've seen pieces in which at least a dozen people were onstage together. These evolve this way:

> Everyone pitches an idea about a theme or a topic.
> Everyone then determines that the idea can be divided into groups or sections. People decide which group, section, or element they want to work on.
> Some people volunteer to direct and/or choreograph their section or the whole event.
> The actors then improvise their section and somehow put it together.
> After they feel they have found the best moments, they script and solidify the piece and rehearse it like clockwork.

PERFORMANCE ART

Cutting off the head of a chicken and slapping its blood on canvas while a woman, perched on a huge block of ice, played the harp is what the term "performance art" meant in the 1960s and 1970s. Today the term is freely used to label any self-generated theatre piece. Performance art is designed to shock, offend, provoke, and "get a rise out of the audience." It sometimes advocates a political position or a social agenda, but more often it unmasks a truth that the audience would prefer to keep denying. Much of it is strong stuff because of its uncompromising nature, but much of it—artists and pieces alike—is possessed with an integrity and a theatricality that deserve to be witnessed.

Example

After each had done his autodrama and was fishing around for a cabaret piece, three Chinese American students decided to develop a work in concert. Their autobiographies interlocked: Each was trying to make it as an actor in the Hollywood market, and each felt a loss of identity along the way. The three men created a piece called *Exit the Dragon** and have taken it on tour to various cities. The material leaves the audience wondering how factual or fictional it is, but the following extracts show how daringly these men use themselves onstage. Some extracts:

Yau: My dad came here for college and he wanted to be an actor. But he was afraid he didn't have enough command of the English language. Then he met my mom, and the responsibility reflex kicked in. All Asian men have it. It's what makes us silent and emotionless.

Eric: Back home we were the only Orientals. It was already embarrassing enough when my friends came into the house. They had to take off their shoes. Or my mom would speak to me in Chinese. Look at those two. My friends would think, "What geeks. They're so Oriental. Why can't they be normal?"

Tuan: No matter where you go, you can find Asians against Asians. They are all American but they choose not to identify with each other.

*Exit the Dragon, created by Eric Zee, Jeff Liu, Yau-gene Chan, and Tuan Tran. Written by Eric Zee.

Eric: (*Covers his face with white makeup.*) Why did I have to be born with this face? I just wanted to be popular with the girls, and there was no way that was going to happen with this face. I would stare in the mirror, and hated what I saw: black hair, slanted eyes and yellow skin. I hated being Chinese. It wasn't fair. Why couldn't I look like everyone else?

Eric: When I visit my relatives in Hong Kong, they make fun of me because I can't speak Chinese and I drink Coke with dinner and I shower in the mornings. I'm not considered Chinese. I'm one of those American born. But if I say I'm an American, they get angry. In America, my friends call me the Chinese guy. I am what you want me to be. I am what you make me.

(ERIC lifts first photo of himself. YAU and TUAN, wearing dark sunglasses, are heard.)

Yau: I want you to be cool. I want you to be athletic. I want you to be a stud. I want you to hold your emotions in.

(ERIC lifts second photo of himself.)

Tuan: I want you to be a good boy. I want you to speak Chinese. I want you to marry a Chinese girl. . . . I want you to kiss ass and exaggerate when necessary.

(YAU and TUAN continue alternating "I want." ERIC shuffles the photos. He screams.)

Eric: I didn't ask to be born Chinese. I didn't ask to grow up in America. I didn't ask to be a minority. I'm not a banana, a wannabe, a computer nerd, a chink. Who I am is not what I am.

RESEARCH PROJECTS

Advocacy for change or critical analysis about the world we are living in is often masked as satire, comedy, or cabaret where the actor is wearing the mask of a character or the facade of an entertainer. No one expects the actor to get on the stage and rant his or her personal view of the world. However actors can and do, out of their concern and passion, invent theatre pieces that are socially relevant and give us a fresh view of what we know, or don't know, or didn't want to know.

The Activist Project

Research
Get to know people who are engaged in some kind of activism. This can be defined as a person who is working to institute change in a very particular way. Examples, political activism, social activism, environmental, medical, educational, and so on. People who are saving animals are activists and so are elementary school teachers helping children through a difficult system.

Observe these people, work alongside them, and become as familiar as you can with their cause. Read any literature, newspaper articles on the work they are doing.

It might be helpful to research people who have an opposing point of view. Study a person who is a pro-life activist and another person who is pro-choice.

What you are working on is doing a real life study of each person. *The person must be passionate and fervent about his or her cause.* You might want to use audiotape or videotape as part of your research. Whether or not you tell your subject what you are doing is up to you. In one case, a student did a study and portrayal of a very famous antiwar activist who was very encouraging about the project. In another case, a male student portrayed a female schoolteacher whom he admired greatly, but like many authors and actors did not want to share that he was using her as a source.

Process

Keep a note book. What is your subject's objective? What are the obstacles? What mistakes do you see him or her making? What do you admire about this person? Could you dedicate your own life to this cause?

If you've been researching two characters who are opposites, finally choose the one who interests you the most.

Sketch out how you see this ten-minute performance piece based on your activist. Bring in impressions, or how the person talks, or a scene the person has told you about. Use others in your group to play other parts, if you need to. Like a one-person show, you are building this one step by step; the only difference is that this is someone else's life, not your own. Slowly, through much trial and error, through trying different material, through seeing what works and what has to be discarded, a shape will emerge.

In conceiving how you intend to put your material on the stage, know you do not have a running time of more than ten minutes. Get all your ideas out, but stay within the final time frame. This will help you not ramble or be redundant, and, in many cases, it will serve to help you be more interesting.

The aim of this project is:

To develop research skills with a degree of thoroughness.
To engage yourself in a life that is fully committed and passionate.
To understand points of view other than your own.
To extend your own acting horizons: you may find a character of the opposite sex interesting enough to portray.
To put an original project on the stage. Or if the facilities exist, have your work videotaped or filmed as a "mockumentary."

The Issues Project

In this instance, the group takes a current issue that is interesting enough to research and explore as a possibility for building a theatre piece. A few years ago when the economy turned and many people were losing their jobs (including the parents of some students), a group decided they would interview people who were unemployed about how their lives were changing and what they had to say. Some of the actors asked, "How am I going to find such people?" Sadly, they were found quite easily—on unemployment lines, through relatives, in bars and restaurants, in church groups, in the same building where students lived, or on the bus. The actors got familiar with many of their stories and found out why and how each person's job was lost.

Some of the actors were able to create a character based on one of their subjects. Other actors put together a composite of several people.

After the actors developed their characterizations, the great question was what to do, how to put these people onstage. Clearly it was time to collaborate with more than each other. Two student directors, who wanted to work in this way, were brought in. The directors split the group and each group devised an hour's presentation that was very powerful.

The advantage of working on something like an activist or issues project is that it brings the world in which we live into our ivory tower of make believe and empowers the actor to be of service to more than himself.

■ || ■ || ■ || ■ || ■ || ■ || ■ || ■ || ■ || ■ || ■ || ■ || ■ || ■ || ■

FREQUENTLY ASKED QUESTIONS

Q: When it comes to a one-person show, how do I start?

A: Start from anywhere. From the middle, from the end, but don't get tied up fretting about the shape of your show. Like a stand-up comic who goes from town to town, club to club, trying out material, the

actor must get up in front of an audience and
do the same act many times. And because everyone's story is different, everyone's way of working
will be different.

Q: When should I have a completed script?

A: Don't script too early. Don't commit yourself to oil
and canvas immediately. Do charcoal sketches first.
Keep them short, under ten minutes. Improvise on
particular topics or characters. Keep it free so you
can find more inspiration when you are playing in
front of an audience. Open yourself to learn from
your audience. It will tell you while you are working
onstage, and many of its members will be glad to tell
you offstage as well.

Q: Shouldn't I use a director to help me get my material
in shape and to serve as an objective eye?

A: Not at first. If after you've performed a good deal of
your material you need someone to help you, fine.
But remember: This is a completely generated actor's
project: book, music, sets, costumes, and starring
you. As soon as you bring in a director, it becomes
a director's project. Try to find someone who will
share the baby with you.

Q: I worry that what I want to do will be offensive. How
far can you go in a cabaret?

A: If the group, say a dozen actors, is putting together
a cabaret, at least two of you should designate yourselves as producers. As producers you oversee everyone's sketches, suggest cuts and staging, and find
ways to get the event performed. The producers
function as quality control and will tell you what
they think. But cabaret shouldn't be homogenized

continued on page 192

continued from page 191

entertainment. It should have teeth and bite. It needn't be safe. Offensive is good. Going too far is good. The only thing you should not do in cabaret is perform badly.

Q: What if I want to do a show and don't want to use material from my own life?

A: That's up to you. You're the one performing. Just make sure that whatever you choose to perform is something that you are very, very passionate about (and that you have the author's rights to).

Q: Aren't one-person shows and cabaret assignments for very advanced students or professionals?

A: I've seen high school students do amazing work in this area. Don't hide behind the excuse of inexperience to keep you from rising to the occasion.

Q: Won't I be yet another actor with a one-man show?

A: Yes. And if you live in Los Angeles you can be yet another person with a screenplay; in New York, yet another person with an idea for a musical. Actors should be proud and willing to empower themselves. All that counts is how good your work is.

Q: What is empowerment?

A: It is not waiting for the phone to ring. It is the actor creating projects and performing them.

Q: What do you think the audience wants to see?

A: Invariably, what will be most effective and theatrical will be the truth of your own experiences. That's what the audience wants to see. That it hasn't seen before.

Q: After I've done most of the work on the activist project, can't I turn it over to a playwright to give it a shape?

A: To "turn it over" is to forfeit your ideas, research, and responsibility. To ask for advice from a playwright is a better idea.

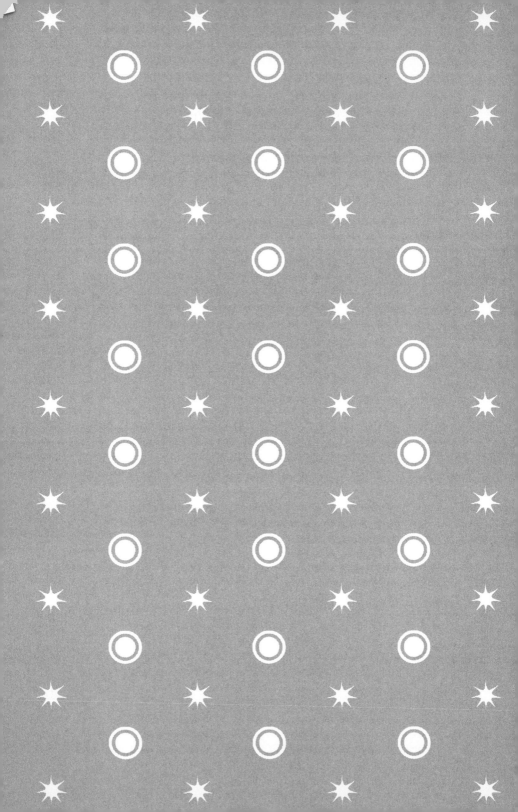

PART V

PERFORMING

Interviews with:

- Ron Leibman

- Laura San Giacomo

- Olympia Dukakis

- Allison Janney

CHAPTER

15

|| ■ || ■ || ■ ||

INTERVIEWS WITH PROFESSIONAL ACTORS ABOUT ACTING

Ron Leibman, Laura San Giacomo, Olympia Dukakis, and Allison Janney were interviewed separately. The discussions centered on performing onstage and their relationship with the audience. We then discussed performing on film and their relationship with the camera. Allison Janney was asked about the differences, if any, between film and stage acting. The reader will see in what these actors say a reflection of what has been presented earlier in this book, but more specifically the reader will see how actors deal with problems and, to a certain extent, how the problems are the same for everyone.

PERFORMING ONSTAGE

Shapiro: What is the day of the performance like for you?
Leibman: [relating to *Angels in America*] My needs for that play were to really stay in bed as long as I could. Today I will go running, but on a day of an *Angels* performance, I didn't run. I would have dinner about 5:00. And most of my day would be spent resting. And very quiet. Reading the paper would be the most . . . trying not to speak on the telephone. Going to the theatre, leaving the house at 6:30, being at the theatre at 7:00, and doing lots of private work with myself, in terms

I wish to thank Rob Leibman, Laura San Giacomo, Olympia Dukakis, and Allison Janney for their contributions.

196

of memory. Because of the nature of the character I was playing. Hopefully I was playing the music correctly. At least playing it the way I and the director and Mr. Kushner had agreed it should be played.

Shapiro: So your warm-up, your preparation, was relaxation and quiet. Did you do any vocal thing before it?

Leibman: Oh, yes, of course I did. When I got to the dressing room. . . . Before my dinner, around 5:30 I would do about a half-hour of ballet exercise and stretches.

Shapiro: This in the dressing room?

Leibman: No. It should be at home. But while I was doing that initial makeup, which took time to put on, I would be doing about twenty minutes of a vocal tape of exercises. To stretch the voice. I always use some kind of vocal warm-up. But this was rather an extensive twenty minutes. Because Roy Cohn [Leibman's character] starts off, he's screaming at people on the phone.

Shapiro: When you're performing a play is your day different?

Dukakis: Yes. Around 3:00, everything begins to fall away. First of all you have to prepare yourself, depending upon what you're doing. Physically, you've got to do exercises, you've got to do stretches, you've got to get your body ready. You've got to try and organize your time so that you are protecting the evening . . . everything is about protecting the evening.

Shapiro: Do you do exercises in the dressing room?

Dukakis: No, I do all that at home. The dressing room . . . I try to have fun with people backstage.

Shapiro: What about performing and your relationship to the audience?

San Giacomo: Well, they are definitely a character in the piece. They will tell you how you're doing all the time. They become part of the rhythm of the play.

Shapiro: What do you do if they're restless?

San Giacomo: Talk louder [laugh]. Sometimes you need to recapture their attention. It's not that I would go outside the given map of the play, or the map of the moment, but there's just an extra something that might come into play.

Shapiro: At what point can you tell what that audience is going to be like?

San Giacomo: I think you can tell once you get out there. And I think the tendency for most actors is either to blame something on the audience or blame it on themselves. That's sort of the two schools. "The audience is terrible tonight" or "What do we do now—they're so quiet."

Shapiro: Who is the audience while you are performing?

Leibman: They are another character. Suddenly, there's another character in the mix. . . . If they're not responding in the way you would like them to respond, it doesn't mean you're off. It doesn't mean you're wrong.

Shapiro: A lot of actors get very angry at an audience, don't they?

Leibman: At one time I thought they were parental substitutes. They're seemingly the authorities of the moment. But if you start unconsciously believing that the audience is your parents who are not being loving to you, then you're going to get very angry. And I think probably that's what happened in my case. I think it was a spillover from childhood, not getting the attention that I wanted.

Shapiro: Who do you play for now?

Leibman: You do it for the fat lady, the one person in that audience whose life might be changed. One of the things that I have learned in recent years because of changes in my own life is I go out for different

reasons now. I didn't used to think about why
I went out. But I realize that. . . . And I really go
out to be of service now, and it's really true. I'm
doing the best I can.

Shapiro: What's been your relationship with the audience?

Dukakis: When you're younger you tend to defend yourself
with the audience. They are the ones that have
been judging you. They are the ones you're trying
to please. You want their approval, you want them
to laugh, and it's a kind of love-hate thing because
when you want and need those things, you'll also
hate the person, the entity that you think has power
over you. Who is the audience? They're unknown.
Well, we know what we do with the unknown. We
project. We make the unknown something. But they
put down their money to have a good time. Not to
stand in judgment of me. Why would somebody put
sixty dollars down to come and judge you? They're
much more selfish and self-centered than that.

Shapiro: What about the actual performance—what's it like
out there?

Leibman: They hate me, I despise them, oh God, oh God,
oh God, I'm dying, I'm dying. I love the next line.
Focus. Focus. Focus. What are you supposed to be
thinking of? Are you supposed to be thinking
about that choice you made? Think about your
mother that time when she said to you . . . and
then get back into it.

There's a great difference between rehearsal
and performance, when they come in the room.
That's a real trick, too. How do you—of course,
you know they're there—but how do you deal
with them and include them without playing to
them? That's experience, I think. I think that's
just a lot of experience. And when you know
you're stepping over the . . . you're digging past

the footlights. . . . do you love me? Do you love me? No, you don't go that far.

Shapiro: It is really mastering so many levels of concentration, isn't it?

Leibman: That's one of the hardest things, and any honest actor will tell you that. Because the performance, a wonderful performance . . . what it takes . . . because great actors, theatre actors in my opinion, always have an awareness of the audience.

Shapiro: And you have to hold for laughs and stay inside the moment, no?

Leibman: Well, if they're laughing a lot you have to take more time, because you've got to wait 'til they finish laughing. But that gives you more time to work on the next thing you want to say or the personalization or the contact with the other actor or a piece of business.

Shapiro: Do you think a competitive spirit is necessary to survive?

Dukakis: You have to want to win. It's the same thing in acting. You have to want your character to win. And presently I see in women's performances, or students', that they haven't learned to fight for their character. Their character's trying to win in the play. They're trying to get everything they want. But that's not something that women are supported in doing. I don't know if you have to have a little more testosterone in you just naturally, or what it is.

At some place the need to be on the stage has to be strong enough to make you take on the nature of the business. The need to do it. Now, there are a lot of people who take on the nature of the business because they want to win, okay, that'll do it. But the trouble is that a lot of very gifted people find it hard to do that. And it's hugely the ones who are extremely gifted and complex human beings who find this a difficult thing to do. And so they're the ones that you worry about.

Shapiro: What if the other actor's performance gets bent out of shape?

Leibman: You can't do anything that night. The lovely thing about the theatre is there's tomorrow. If you're diplomatic and loving, you take the person aside and you say, do you know, from my experience, let's, maybe next time . . . and you include yourself, you say I was pushing tonight. When they were pushing. The last thing you want to do is make them defensive, "What do you mean I was pushing?" You say, I think I was pushing. You know what I'm going to try next time? Maybe we should both do this, is let's get quieter next time, because the audience is never going to come to us if we keep pushing. And I think it was my fault, when you know it was their fault. And generally, they'll come along. Unless they're very inexperienced and think they're doing one thing and they're really not. Then you're in trouble.

Shapiro: What does frighten you about acting?

San Giacomo: Every first night of a play I think, "Why am I doing this? Why did I get myself into this? I hate this. I'm scared. I don't want to go out there."

Shapiro: Just the first night?

San Giacomo: The first, maybe second night. And after that you get into the rhythm of the piece and then you go: "What was I scared of? This is so much fun!"

Shapiro: I often think why people go to the theatre is to see and hear a good story. Do you agree?

Dukakis: Well, I don't know what else it's about. In some ways you have to want to tell a story. You have to want to be a storyteller. I think rehearsal for the stage is like a kind of trying to find out what the parameters are. To kind of figure out . . . for me it's how can I tell the story.

ACTING IN FILM

Shapiro: Is the preparation different for film?

San Giacomo: In rehearsal for a play, you're always moving forward bit by bit by bit, and something does change when you get in front of an audience. But in film, there's usually not any rehearsal, so . . . I've done as much work as I can by myself, in plotting the emotional arc of the character. Where do I think her moments are? What is each scene about?

Shapiro: In film do you feel you have to be more prepared?

San Giacomo: Not necessarily.

Shapiro: But in a play you're rehearsing slowly, evolving, you're gestating, you have a sense of progression . . .

San Giacomo: What's miraculous is that in film you don't have that, but yet you're able to do the same thing. Maybe sometimes better because it's so impromptu and spontaneous.

Shapiro: How is the use of yourself different?

San Giacomo: You can't rehearse too much. That's one thing you cannot do.

Shapiro: Okay, what is it?

San Giacomo: I feel like no matter how much you rehearse, you get there on the day and it's always different. Let's say, you rehearse for two weeks before you shoot a film. Depending on the type of material it is, two weeks may be too much. So that's in October. In November you go to shoot a scene. You get to the location, and it's absolutely different. You could have this whole elaborate thing worked out about how you're going to be on the phone and how you're going to go like this, and you're going to look towards the camera, and it's going to be really cool because you're going to be getting really intimate and then you're there, and they'll say, "Okay, sit." You can't move. Because we've got this fabulous light back here and the camera is going to move.

Also, I find, the work that I do is more intimate in film. I find I will take more dangerous areas of who I am. More private than something I'm going to work with for a month or two on a play. It's got to be something that's going to work for me every night for two months. And it's got to be a technique that's going to hold up for two months. But for a film, if you're working on it for six hours, it's over. So you've got to get there fast.

In a film, you don't have the play to wind around you. You have the character that's sitting with you for a month and a half. But you don't have any of the life around it. So then you've got to go to something even deeper, something even more personal. In a film if I have to get to the moment where I have to cry with this person or have this real intimate moment, what I find is extremely helpful is it has got to happen with the person I'm working with. Because that's the most present you can be. You can't deal with substitution. I mean, for years I tried to do this stupid substitution thing. I'm sorry, Uta Hagen. But it has to be about the sufferings in you. It has to be about you. And that's really scary. It has to be pertaining to the scene and about what really happens. I have to be in character, in this person talking to this other character, this person, this actor. It has to be completely of the moment. As long as it's connected with the scene and with that other person, then it works. For me.

Shapiro: Would Ron Leibman's Roy Cohn be different on film?

Leibman: I would do exactly the same work but wouldn't have to talk as loud. Roy Cohn would be exactly the same except . . . energy level down. You've got to fill a 1,500-seat theatre, for instance, as compared to filling the screen.

Shapiro: What about performing for the camera?

Leibman: If you don't know that camera's there, then you belong in an institution. If you don't know the audience is there, you belong in an institution. You have what someone once called "a third ear." You are operating in front of an audience on so many levels. In the theatre, if you are just doing the scene very quietly, you're not, really. You're getting extra air, which you don't need in front of the camera. That would look awful. A lot of stage actors have not made or cannot make the transition because they don't get it. It's just a smaller room.

Shapiro: What are the essential differences for you?

Leibman: When you're onstage at 8:00 you can't stop.

Shapiro: What are the difficulties in performing for film?

Leibman: One of the great frustrations of filmmaking . . . some actors say, well, you shoot out of sequence. That's not the problem. The problem is some of your best work is taken out, not because they were bad, but because the director felt we should be on him now or on you now. Films are . . . someone said, they're movies. They have to move. It's very different. You don't need as much dialogue. They also cut all the time.

Shapiro: Do you like performing for the camera?

San Giacomo: I like the camera. You have to know where it is because you can't be doing some great unconscious movement. You have to know where your stage is.

Shapiro: Do you always know where the shot is? What the shot is going to be?

San Giacomo: I went through a period where occasionally I would find out where it was, but mostly I would just do my thing because it was so new to me. And just keep it small. I knew that when it was really close I would have to tone some things down. Now I'm always trying to find out where it is. Now I'm trying to go through a more conscious period of always knowing where it is so that if I want to do something . . . for instance, I did this scene and I loved this unconscious moment where she has finished her drink, and she puts her fist in the glass, and you don't know what she's going to do. But then I realized it was all below camera, and I was kind of upset. At that point there's no way you can lift it up. So I think one can use where the camera is to help you. That's your stage.

Shapiro: Is that who you perform for in film—the camera? Or do you perform for the director or yourself . . . what's the audience there?

San Giacomo: Well, I don't really feel like I'm performing for the camera. I feel the camera is watching, but I feel that I have to be present with the other actor in the scene first and foremost. The camera is like a voyeur. It's almost like what happens with an audience in that there's the triangle going on except the camera doesn't give you the feedback. And also you don't have the same kind of a relationship with the camera. The camera always makes me want to be really intimate.

Shapiro: What about skills?

Dukakis: I think it's incredibly important to think of yourself as skilled . . . because you have to really wrap your head around a lot of technical things. You have to be able to play a scene several different ways. Someone says, okay, play the scene another way, and you have to be able to take what you might think is the character and begin to turn that dial inside you to all sorts of gradations. You have to do that with an action. You have to do that with an obstacle. And you have to do it on your toes. In film the director is looking constantly for the composition. And he's not certain

until he gets in the editing room which way that
story is going to go.

Shapiro: For example . . . ?

Dukakis: "Can you do this, but keep your voice up higher?"
We know in the theatre that everything . . . who you
are and what actions you're choosing to do affect
where your voice goes. Say your voice happens
to go into your chest. He says, "That's good, but
your voice is too low. Can you keep it up higher?"
You can do that technically. You just think,
"Okay, bring my voice higher." But . . . and this is
an example of working from the outside in, if
I choose to make my voice higher, that already will
change how I'll behave with you.

Shapiro: Do you know what the shot will look like?

Dukakis: You have to really listen closely and watch closely
and ask questions about what the director is doing
with the camera. You've got to really know.

Shapiro: And that tempers the performance?

Dukakis: It certainly tempers the manner of the articulation of what you're doing. I think it sometimes
tempers choices. You may think of a moment
as being wild, but if what the director wants is
a real . . . he's coming in close for that . . . you've
got to figure something else. How much. . . . So
you better ask what the camera's doing, where
it's going. How does he see it ultimately? You try
to get as much information about how he's
shooting it.

Shapiro: Were you ever frightened of the camera?

Dukakis: I was terrified. I suppose I was nervous. Nervous
doesn't address what I felt.

Shapiro: Do you see dailies and things like that?

Dukakis: No. I cannot watch myself because I become too . . .
I scrutinize myself too strongly.

Shapiro: What about your first film?

Dukakis: The director [Jules Dassin] auditioned me for a whole day. A whole day we talked of this and that. He hired me, we go to the set, in three minutes, he dropped down to me and said, "You don't like the camera." I was caught. And I admitted it.

He said, "Why don't you like the camera?" I said, "I feel that it's totally controlling me. And people have been telling me that I'm too big for this thing . . . " He said to me, "Acting is acting. You do whatever you want. I'll move this thing. It's just a piece of equipment, a thing." I said, "Really, I can go anywhere I want?" He said, "Anywhere." He asked if I could feel the lights. He made me walk around. I said, "I guess I can feel like the camera's seeing everything, like my nose, or my . . . the things that I feel are too big, too small, too this, too that, you know, and that the camera will see everything." He said, "It will see everything." He wasn't letting me off the hook. In other words, what he was saying was you don't withdraw your vulnerability because of that. I tell you, this man I got to trust so much. He came up to me at one point and said, "Do you know in Greece when they interrogate women they take their clothes off?" I looked, and I said, "You want me to take my clothes off in this scene I've been playing?" And now he's telling me, "Yes, would you do it?" I said, "If you tell me that this is necessary and you want it," I said, "yes, I'll do it."

Shapiro: Do the retakes become your preparation?

Dukakis: In a way they do.

Shapiro: And rehearsal?

Dukakis: I have worked with two-week rehearsal periods. Even three days makes an incredible difference. *Moonstruck* was two weeks. *Dad,* two weeks. *Steel*

Magnolias, two weeks. If you really pay attention . . .
I make a big deal about this paying attention . . .
but you've got to know what the hell's happening.
You better try and figure out what the rules of
the games are because they change with directors
and actors and material. You've got to really be on
your toes. You can't be wedded to any particular
way of working. What I think we really need is to
become very skillful at many, many things so that
we can involve ourselves in different ways of working. Actors are chameleons, we are constantly transforming ourselves to do this, to do that. I find
this much more exciting than standing there
saying, "This is how I work" and raising the banner
of truth.

SOME DIFFERENCES BETWEEN FILM AND STAGE ACTING

Shapiro: Acting in film, acting on the stage—what's the
difference?

Janney: Acting on the stage is a team sport and, yet, just
because you're not talking or it's not your moment
doesn't mean your presence is not needed to fulfill
the other actor's moment. That you must give focus
to that actor; so you're always on whether you're
speaking or not.

In film, the editor gets to cut things together
where you're not always on camera. There are
those actors who, when they are not on camera,
don't always give their all. Maybe they're on
the freeway on their way home and their stand-in
is giving their lines, or an actor is sick and has to
go home and you are acting with a stand-in.
Things like that happen all the time.

I think that your focus is challenged a lot
when you are doing movies because there are so

many people around you all the time, poking at you, fixing your make-up, fussing with your clothes, getting ready for the shot, screaming around you . . . it becomes a challenge to keep focus and concentrate on the scene. It just uses different muscles.

Shapiro: What's the difference in how you prepare?

Janney: I love the luxury of preparing for stage. That time of rehearsal where you get to mess up and discover things and change things, I long for that, because it's so precious. There are some directors like Sam Mendes, who had a rehearsal period for a week or so for *American Beauty*. We all sat around and read through the script. We started off the day reading through the script and then he would break down the scene and work with the actors. He comes from the theatre so maybe that's why he had to work that way, but I think it was beneficial to everyone, because the actors felt like they were in the same movie. Whereas, when you do something like *West Wing* and episodic you get to show up and know your lines and you maybe will get a ten-minute rehearsal if you're lucky. You just have to trust that you got the part because you are the character or you know what you're doing, because they don't give you a lot of time to find anything when you're doing that kind of work. A lot of movies too that I have been cast in have been similar: you show up and they block the scene and you do it. There is no rehearsal and your preparation is all at home, and you better come knowing your lines.

Shapiro: Do you find that you have more freedom in the theatre?

Janney: Absolutely. That's what I miss the most about stage acting. When the curtain goes up that part is mine and no one is going to stop me, or tell me to change it, or how I should do it. That was what the rehearsal process was for. But every night is going to be different, and you own it and it's your part. An editor can't come in and cut out a moment he didn't like. It's yours and it's pure and I miss that. In film you have no control. All you can do is your best work every time and hope that your moments will be on screen.

Shapiro: Back to how you prepare. Talk about your role in *The West Wing.*

Janney: It depends on what the scene is. If it's an emotional scene, I'll just listen to music or I have to go off in my head and fantasize about wherever I need to be emotionally. It may have nothing to do with what the scene is about, but I think about whatever I need to put me in a place that has the right emotions for what the scene requires. If the scene does it itself, then I don't need to prepare, it's fantastic. There have been a couple of scenes where I knew what they were without having to search for it, but there's times I don't get it or I'm not feeling it that day and I have to go some place in my mind to get that emotion and then just forget the preparation, and go do the work in the scene and hopefully it will bring up what I just prepared for.

Shapiro: And when you were in the Broadway revival of *A View From the Bridge,* how did you prepare for those performances?

Janney: There are some actors who can just turn their emotions on and off so easily and I wasn't like that; I had to come to the theater an hour and half early and just do my preparation and then do little mini-preparations throughout the performance, especially for this one scene in the second act.

Shapiro: What scene was that?

Janney: That was the Christmas scene where I just had to be so raw emotionally. It scared me every night to go out there. Some nights I couldn't find the emotions and I felt like a doctor who had lost a patient on the operating table. I felt so upset that I couldn't do it. I gave what I could, but I didn't feel comfortable pretending to cry, so my character would be very stoic that night, which was not where I wanted her to be.

On a performance day I would look for anything, on the bus, on the way to work, I'd see an image of someone who touched me and I'd remember that. I take—I mean I was like a sponge, looking for anything to take with me on stage that night because that's all I had—my experiences that day and how I felt that day. That play drained me every day just thinking about the performance and hoping that night it would come easily to me, but it didn't come easily to me. It was very difficult.

Shapiro: What's the most important aspect of training you would suggest to students?

Janney: I have always said that listening is the most important thing you can do in acting. A lot of people aren't good listeners and those are the people who are not fun to act with, and aren't fun to watch. I just want to tell people to stop acting and just listen.

Shapiro: What about characterizing?

Janney: If I stumble upon a character, it's not because of a conscious choice of mine to become a character. I'll hook into something that is related to me. I remember going to London once and studying and I got very upset that the teacher said I shouldn't drag the character down to my level; I should aspire to the character. That didn't work

for me. I still drag the character down to my level.
No matter who it is, they're going to be some part
of me. Just start with yourself, at least, and then
add things, the exterior things that make you not
Allison Janney, not who you are, but who the character is. Start with yourself.

AN AFTERWORD

THE AUTHOR INTERVIEWS HIMSELF

Q: Have you said everything you wanted to on the
subject?

A: Considering that I had always believed that what
I do couldn't be put in a book, I'd say I've said
most of it.

Q: Did you impress on them the need to read? Did you
let them know that so many actors out there don't
know the repertoire, don't know the history of
theatre, have no frame of reference to anything
beyond what they watch on television? Did you
hammer this home?

A: I stressed the need for the actor to read, to know his
or her business, to do research, yes. But I can't say
I hammered it.

Q: At least did you hammer home the fact that actors
need a . . . way of working? They have to stop standing in front of their teacher and their directors
waiting for someone to magic them. In other words,
do all the work for them?

A: I showed them tools, I went through the
process, I encouraged them to do their own
work, yes.

Q: What about their using their own imagination?
I hope you stressed that.

A: It's the core of the book.

continued on page 214

continued from page 213

Q: I hope you laid it on about empowerment. How actors should stop being wet noodles, waiting for the phone to ring. How they should start their own group, reader's theatre, develop their own cabarets, one-person shows, do performance art, and so on.

A: I laid it all out, yes.

Q: But I bet you didn't hammer them home, right?

A: I'm not a hammerer.

Q: What haven't you said? What's the last thing you'd like to leave them with?

A: Courage. Have heart. Believe in yourself. Do it for the love of it. That's all.

INDEX

215